Finish Your
Dissertation
ONCE AND FOR ALL!

Finish Your Dissertation

ONCE AND FOR ALL!

How to Overcome Psychological Barriers, Get Results, and Move on With Your Life

ALISON B. MILLER

American Psychological Association
Washington, DC

First Printing, October 2008
Second Printing, August 2012

Published by
American Psychological Association
750 First Street, NE
Washington, DC 20002
www.apa.org

To order
APA Order Department
P.O. Box 92984
Washington, DC 20090-2984
Tel: (800) 374-2721; Direct: (202) 336-5510
Fax: (202) 336-5502; TDD/TTY: (202) 336-6123
Online: www.apa.org/books/
E-mail: order@apa.org

In the U.K., Europe, Africa, and the Middle East, copies may be ordered from
American Psychological Association
3 Henrietta Street
Covent Garden, London
WC2E 8LU England

Typeset in Meridien by Circle Graphics, Columbia, MD

Printer: Data Reproductions, Auburn Hills, MI
Cover Designer: Naylor Design, Washington, DC

Technical/Production Editor: Kathryn Funk

The opinions and statements published are the responsibility of the authors, and such opinions and statements do not necessarily represent the policies of the American Psychological Association.

Library of Congress Cataloging-in-Publication Data

Library of Congress Cataloging-in-Publication Data

Miller, Alison B.
  Finish your dissertation once and for all! : how to overcome psychological barriers, get results, and move on with your life / Alison B. Miller. — 1st ed.
    p. cm.
  Includes bibliographical references and index.
  ISBN-13: 978-1-4338-0415-1
  ISBN-10: 1-4338-0415-8
 1. Dissertations, Academic — Authorship. 2. Academic writing — Psychological aspects. I. Title.

  LB2369.M454 2009
  808'.02—dc22   2008023405

British Library Cataloguing-in-Publication Data
A CIP record is available from the British Library.

Printed in the United States of America
First Edition

Contents

Preface

Finish Your Dissertation Once and for All! is a book I have imagined for many years. As a doctoral student in clinical psychology, I had the sense that the experience of being a graduate student could be better. I began my first year of graduate school feeling excited to begin a new chapter in my life, conduct research, and learn to become a clinician. Yet my excitement quickly gave way to fear—the fear that I was neither intelligent enough nor worthy enough to earn a doctoral degree and that I had "tricked" the faculty into admitting me into the program. Worst of all, I feared that somewhere along the way I would possibly fail to earn a PhD. This fear diminished my yearning to learn, my capacity to use my actual intellectual abilities, my willingness to delve deeply into academics, and my enthusiasm for school. Graduate school became something I had to survive.

It is not as if I believed that I had no intellectual skills or abilities at all. I knew that I had to possess some degree of competence to be admitted into a graduate program. There were even times when I felt good about my intellectual abilities. Yet those times of confidence were fleeting, giving way to the fear that if I was not careful, I would be exposed as a fraud who was undeserving of a PhD. My fears led to a significant problem in my early years of graduate school: procrastination.

While I was working on my master's thesis, my problem with procrastination became acute. I developed a bad habit of watching *The Real World* on MTV. In case you are not familiar with it, *The Real World* is a reality television show about the drama, conflict, and romantic relationships of seven young adults living together in a house for several months. On the weekends, MTV frequently aired marathons of *The Real World* showing episode after half-hour episode all day long. I would never start a Saturday or Sunday planning to watch TV, but inevitably I would end up on the couch. Only one, I would tell myself, but one episode would become two, then three, and even four, and the next thing I knew, the better part of the day was gone. Even if I managed to turn off the television, I was able to procrastinate with some other activity (laundry, talking on the phone, and eating were some of my favorite procrastination activities).

One day in mid-October, with a department deadline looming, I had had enough of my bad work habits. I made a declaration to myself that the procrastination had to end. I went to my office, sat at the computer, and began to work on my master's thesis. Yet after only 1 hour, I found myself in the hallway of my apartment on the way to the couch, eyeing the remote control. Like so many times before, I was in the midst of procrastination, not knowing how or why it was happening. Only this time something different happened. I caught myself in the act. I actually paused in the hallway and asked myself, "How did I get here?" I had no recollection of making a conscious decision to stop writing, to get up from my desk, or to head for the television.

This was an *aha!* moment for me. I recognized what had preceded my latest attempt to avoid my thesis writing: The work had become difficult. Just before I ended up in the hallway, I had become confused about how to organize and express my ideas and findings. This confusion left me feeling anxious and fearful that I was not smart enough. Thus, I actively avoided my thesis as a way to avoid feeling what I did not want to feel. That morning I had three very important realizations. One, I realized that I was confusing being stuck and uncertain with lacking intelligence. Two, the behavior I used to escape the anxiety and fear of being intellectually inadequate was preventing me from fully engaging in my work and pushing myself academically and intellectually. Three, my anxiety and fear and the behavior I used to cope were preventing me from doing what I came to graduate school to do: to learn.

This moment of insight was when I recognized and understood how my fear that I was not intelligent had come to define me and was actually preventing me from pushing through and persevering in the face of intellectual challenges. In the days after this event, I began envisioning another way to approach my graduate work. This new way, I imagined, could involve far less procrastination and a much greater willingness to work, even when it was a struggle.

Over time I developed a more structured, systematic approach to academic work that provided me with time to struggle, write rough drafts, and ask for help. Also, I deliberately planned meaningful time off from graduate work so I would be less likely to binge on *The Real World* or indulge in other distractions. By the time I conducted my dissertation, I had developed a project management approach that became the foundation of the dissertation coaching services I provide.

Over the past decade, I have worked as a dissertation coach helping thousands of graduate students individually and in groups. A "dissertation coach?" you might be asking yourself. "What is that?" Following a growing profession of executive and life coaches in the United States, a number of people began providing a new service in the late 1990s focused on coaching graduate students to successfully propose and defend their doctoral dissertations. Over the past 10 years, the number of dissertation coaches, although still small, has grown consistently. Type "dissertation coach" into any search engine on the Internet, and you will find quite a few individuals who provide this service. The services they offer vary but focus largely on helping graduate students overcome procrastination, sustain motivation, and create a sound plan for completing their dissertation. Dissertation coaches also provide accountability, serve as a sounding board for research ideas, help students solve dissertation-related problems, and offer support that many students do not find in their doctoral programs. My intention is to provide graduate students with much of the information, ideas, and strategies I offer to my own clients. You can think of this book as your very own dissertation coach.

Acknowledgments

Writing a book is a challenging endeavor. In the end, though, writing this book has been a remarkable journey of learning, persistence, and patience, and I feel that the task has left me a better person. I must start by thanking all of the thousands of graduate students I have had the chance to work with as clients and as participants in dissertation workshops since 2000. I have learned so much from you about what it really takes to finish a doctoral dissertation, and I have been inspired by so many of you who took bold action in the direction of completing your dissertations, even when it was difficult or frightening.

I also thank Lansing Hays, who for several years politely insisted that I write a book proposal and believed that I was the right person to write this book. Thank you to Linda McCarter for seamlessly taking over the reins from Lansing and urging me to "just write the book" and turn it in for review. I am forever in gratitude to Margaret (Peggy) Sullivan, my development editor at the American Psychological Association, who believed in the vision and message of this book and helped me to improve my work in a number of important ways. Peggy, your thoughtful commentary and insights were indispensable. I appreciate your support and wisdom a great deal. I am thankful to Tyler Aune for his help with permissions and the business side of book publishing, to Judy Nemes for coming in toward the end of my revision process and helping me get to the finish line, and to Kathryn Funk for effectively overseeing the production of this book. Also, I am grateful to Sue Morris for her very helpful copyediting and suggestions to improve the book, especially chapter 1. Thank you to Bernadette Sanchez for her help with chapters 5 and 7 and for being a great friend and a true role model of a great dissertation advisor. Thank you to Marina Tolou-Shams for her support and contributions to chapter 4 and, of course, for her friendship.

I also greatly appreciate the support and ideas from Christopher Keys (Christopher, you were a great advisor and role model for many of the things I discuss in this book), Roger Weissberg, and Olga Reyes for their ideas regarding the focus and content of chapter 7. Roger, I must also thank you for leading me to the work of Carol Dweck, which has been critical to the development of my dissertation coaching approach. Thank you to Tamar Heller. Although you were not involved directly in writing this book, you are the person who gave me the chance to write early on in my graduate career and who taught me so much about writing. Thank you to Albert Ellis (who passed away as I was writing this book), Carol Dweck, Steven Hayes, Jinny Ditzler, and their colleagues for their brilliant research and ideas that made my approach to coaching doctoral students and this book possible. Your work has affected me in a very deep sense both personally and professionally and enabled me, in turn, to help others personally and professionally.

I am grateful for my "play group" friends, Anneliese, Beth, India, Jennifer, Joanne, Laura, Mary Catherine, and Susie, for being there every Friday with a glass of wine waiting. Knowing there was a place to relax and unwind in the throes of writing this book made a real difference. I love each and every one of you, and I greatly appreciate our community of women, husbands, and children. Thank you to Carolyn Baba and Helen Nodland for your incredible friendship, support, and belief in me as a writer. I love you both very much. Thanks to the remarkable "mojo repair" coaching and consulting group of Amy, Beth, Betsy, Cheryl, Lee, James, Jennifer, Jeremy, Peg, and Thea for your ongoing support as I wrote this book and in all other personal and professional matters. You are the best partners I could ask for. I am grateful to have such a loving brother, Jeremy, and parents, Dalia and Kip, who have always had faith in my potential.

I am forever grateful to my husband, Ray, who lovingly endured living with someone writing a book. I appreciate all of the support and time you gave me to focus on bringing this project to fruition. Thanks for being on the journey with me and for being a great partner and husband. I love you deeply. And thank you to my incredible kids, Emma and Aidan. Emma told me recently, "Mom, you've been writing this book my whole life." Not quite, but close. I love you both. I hope to instill many of the ideas in this book in your education long before you end up in graduate school (not that I am pushing graduate school).

Finally, I would like to acknowledge myself for the achievement of writing this book. Writing a book to help graduate students finish their dissertations was a huge undertaking in the context of a very full life. I persevered to bring this book into existence, and I am proud of my accomplishment. I hope that my readers will take my lead and acknowledge themselves along the way and at the end of earning a doctoral degree.

Finish Your
Dissertation

ONCE AND FOR ALL!

Introduction

Are you having difficulty finishing your dissertation? Are you feeling stuck after trying various ways to approach your topic or to write one or more chapters? Do you have doubts that you will *ever* finish, no matter how well you know your topic and your methodology? Are you feeling panicky about the entire enterprise or at least parts of it? If so, it is unlikely that your cognitive abilities are to blame. More likely, the culprits are anxiety, self-doubt, procrastination, perfectionism, and the thoughts, feelings, and behavior that accompany these difficulties. This book was written to help you overcome these problems and finish your dissertation once and for all.

Over the past decade, I have worked as a dissertation coach helping thousands of graduate students like you, both individually and in groups. I have developed a scientifically based strategy that will help you address the emotional, behavioral, and cognitive issues that keep you stuck. However, I will not burden you unnecessarily with theory and research (although I will provide citations for those who are interested in the science behind my approach). I will coach you in practical terms, just as I would if we were sitting together in my office, your living room, or a coffee shop.

I came by the approach described in this book honestly. That is, I too was once stuck in a quagmire of self-doubt that kept me paralyzed and unable to progress in graduate school, despite my intellectual ability to do so. I was able to see myself out of the quagmire, and since then I have successfully helped many students make it to the PhD finish line. I hope to help you, too.

What to Expect From This Book

In this book, I provide a structured yet flexible approach based on my coaching practice. I offer specific, tangible strategies that you can use to determine the behavior, emotions, and thinking that you can change and learn to manage what you cannot change so that you are more productive, motivated, and equipped to successfully complete your dissertation. In short, I will be your personal coach as you tackle obstacles and succeed beyond your own expectations. I believe the material in this book is needed for many graduate students. If you have picked up this book, it is likely it can help you wherever you are on the dissertation journey.

The book is geared primarily toward students in the social sciences, as most of the examples of how graduate students can apply the principles in this book are in those fields. Yet I have successfully used these strategies with students in the life sciences, physical sciences, and the humanities as well. For the sake of readability, I use the term *PhD* synonymously with *doctoral degree*. However, I realize that even in my own field, psychology, there are doctoral degrees that go by other names such as PsyD (doctor of professional psychology) or EdD (doctor of education). Also, students can use the approach and strategies in this book at any stage of their graduate education, whether they are taking courses, writing a master's thesis, preparing for comprehensive exams, or completing a dissertation. Although the focus of this book is on dissertations, I believe many students will benefit from reading it early in their graduate career.

I want to emphasize that this book is about the approach you take to doing your dissertation. It is not a book that focuses on the specific content of dissertations or how to conduct a sound dissertation study generally or in a particular field (e.g., see Cone & Foster, 2006). Other texts offer good advice on how to conduct a dissertation, thesis, or other academic research. These texts focus on matters such as developing a research topic, writing literature reviews, methodology and study design, quantitative and qualitative data analysis, and presenting and discussing findings. Many of my clients have used such books to help them as they developed their dissertation proposals and carried out their dissertation study. Time and time again, however, I have been asked by clients and students who attend my workshops to write a book that addresses how students can improve the way they approach their dissertation. They tell me that a book is needed to help students learn to create a sound, structured approach to completing their dissertations and to help them better deal with the negative thoughts, feelings, and behavior that so frequently accompany the experience of doing a dissertation. This book is an effort to honor their request.

Roadmap for This Book

I hope this book will offer you support, guidance, and reassurance in graduate school and on your dissertation journey. In the first three chapters, you will learn about the intellectual and psychological challenges of completing a dissertation and how you can find your way through these challenges. The last five chapters focus on more tangible behavioral strategies that you can use to bring your dissertation to completion.

Chapter 1 will help you understand what makes a dissertation so challenging and how you can reconnect with your values and use the inherent challenge of completing a dissertation to learn important lessons and experience personal growth. You will also learn to reconnect with your real purpose for seeking a doctoral degree.

Chapter 2 reviews the common thinking, feeling, and behaving traps frequently experienced by doctoral students. This chapter will help you recognize thoughts, feelings, and behaviors that diminish motivation and productivity and that fuel procrastination, avoidance, and perfectionism. In addition, you will learn how thoughts, feelings, and behavior influence and reinforce each other, often making it difficult to break free from these traps.

Chapter 3 offers you a variety of strategies to free yourself from thinking, feeling, and behaving traps. The aim of this chapter is to help you change the thoughts and feelings that can be changed and to develop a more accepting stance toward those thoughts and feelings that are difficult to change. The chapter will also teach you how you can change your behavior to take bold action consistent with your values and to make progress on your dissertation.

Chapters 4 and 5 teach you how to use a structured, project management approach to actively manage your energy and the process of carrying out a dissertation study. In chapter 4, you will learn how to create timelines to plan how you will complete particular stages of your dissertation over time. In chapter 5, you will learn to break down your larger timeline goals into daily action plans that provide great specificity about the work you need to do on a day-to-day basis.

Chapter 6 focuses specifically on strategies to help you write and revise your dissertation more effectively. You will learn strategies to increase your motivation and productivity even when you are feeling stuck or overwhelmed. Chapter 7 offers guidance on working well with your chairperson and committee members and having successful proposal and final dissertation-defense meetings. Finally, chapter 8 makes a case for actively taking care of yourself and giving yourself time to rest and enjoy life as you work on your dissertation. It is my hope that the focus of chapter 8, as well as much of the other material in this book, will be useful in life beyond the doors of graduate school.

Many of the chapters contain exercises that reinforce key lessons, ideas, and strategies to help you be successful and even experience personal growth and joy as you earn a PhD. As you conduct your dissertation, I encourage you to revisit the chapters of this book you find helpful in your first reading.

I am eternally optimistic that no matter how much you have put your dissertation off, how fearful or demoralized you feel, how long it has been since you spoke with your chairperson, or how much you doubt you will finish, there is a way to succeed, finish your dissertation once and for all, and earn the doctoral degree you are seeking. I have seen so many students overcome seemingly insurmountable difficulties to make it to the finish line. You can cross the finish line, too. I wish you the best on your dissertation journey. I am rooting for you!

The Doctoral Dissertation
A Dual Challenge
1

The dissertation is the final and usually the most challenging hurdle that stands between students and their being awarded a doctoral degree. Successfully completing a dissertation for typical graduate students is one of the most demanding experiences of their lives, at least their academic lives. As you work on your dissertation, you may find yourself struggling at times with ideas, concepts, writing, motivation, self-doubt, negative emotions, and the stamina required to complete a project of this magnitude. Yet these struggles offer you the opportunity to learn, grow as a person, and stretch yourself intellectually, psychologically, and creatively.

Most important, I believe completing a dissertation offers you the opportunity to experience the joy that comes from being able to stay engaged and present when difficulties arise. Often we have learned to dislike not knowing the answers to academic challenges or to back away when solutions are not readily apparent. Yet your dissertation experience can be a time in your life when you learn to love and appreciate challenges for the growth in competence and capacities they foster, the life experiences they grant, and the wisdom they impart.

What Makes a Doctoral Dissertation So Difficult?

Most books on completing your dissertation address the technical or intellectual challenges that such a task presents. However, I believe that it is important to acknowledge that there is another challenge inherent in completing a doctoral dissertation, and that challenge is personal. Completing such dissertation tasks tests not only the intellectual abilities but also the personality of the graduate student. By this I mean that the dissertation will bring out any emotional, behavioral, or thinking issues that the student has (and we all have issues) and challenge him or her to face them and succeed. This is why I consider completing the dissertation a dual challenge.

The Intellectual Challenge

Doctoral dissertations are challenging by design. A doctorate in an academic field, whether it is in the humanities or the social, life, or physical sciences, is the highest-ranking degree offered by academic institutions. To earn this degree, universities require that students complete a dissertation study. This requirement is designed to be a test of the student's ability to conduct independent scholarly work and formulate conclusions that will either change or expand previous research findings or knowledge (Yale University, 1975). There may be some exceptions to this standard, but successfully completing a dissertation is the final, universal admission ticket to earning a PhD. The dissertation process is designed to be rigorous and intellectually challenging. If it were easy to complete a dissertation and earn a PhD, wouldn't far more people pursue this degree?

Although I hope your dissertation chair and your committee give you input and guidance as you work on your dissertation, you are expected to dedicate yourself to this project with a high degree of independence. In the academic world, the dissertation study is viewed as an important means for students to demonstrate their competence and capacity for carrying out sound research. Most students have never undertaken a research project of this stature or scope, at least not in an independent manner. Thus, the dissertation is usually experienced as highly intellectually challenging. It often pushes people to stretch themselves and go beyond their perceived limitations.

Another challenging aspect of conducting a dissertation is that it is often seen as threatening to a student's identity as an intelligent person. Doctoral students are, by and large, a group of people who believe that being intelligent and being able to perform well in an academic arena are important. Being intelligent is a significant part of their identity and is something they value highly. Therefore, demonstrating competence and being viewed as intelligent are essential sources of motivation in the lives of most graduate students. There is nothing wrong with placing such an emphasis on intellect (although I would dissuade you from believing that intellect is more important than other human capacities and qualities). We obviously need to have people in this world who care about their intelligence and who use their intellect to further knowledge, make discoveries, develop theories, and bring about positive change. Yet the way the dissertation process is designed is bound to make most students feel anxious and wonder whether they possess the intellectual skills and capacity they need to finish their degree.

At many points during the dissertation process answers and solutions do not come easily and the next steps of what to research, write, or analyze are not obvious. It is important to remember that many, if not most, academic research endeavors require some intellectual struggle even for experienced faculty. These struggles may be even more challenging for students who, by definition, are in a stage of life where they are apprentices learning to become independent academics and professionals. Consequently, their academic work will be critiqued as part of their "apprenticeship." Students often interpret their academic struggles and being challenged, questioned, and critiqued as signs of intellectual inadequacy instead of important vehicles for growth and the development of knowledge, skills, and capacities.

This interpretation is unfortunate because it leads many graduate students to become fearful of the very work they came to do in graduate school. For example, you may have to work harder to understand statistics or struggle with some aspects of writing. These challenges are not the same as being intellectually inferior or incapable of learning, developing skills, or earning a PhD. They do mean that you might have to work harder in some areas. You may need to ask for more help, do extra reading, or more carefully and methodically learn how to carry out a particular aspect of research. As you will learn by reading this book, needing to work harder is not the same as being unintelligent.

The Personal Challenge

Virtually all graduate students face stress-related problems at some point during the dissertation process. Such difficulties can be both the cause and the effect of cognitive, emotional, and behavioral roadblocks. For example, students often have beliefs or thoughts that they are not smart enough to complete a PhD. The most common negative emotion I have witnessed is anxiety, as students realize the enormity of the dissertation and cannot see how the project can be broken up into manageable chunks. The most common behavioral manifestation is procrastination, when students avoid their dissertation work as a way to avoid the unpleasant thoughts and feelings associated with doing the work. When cognitive, behavioral, and emotional difficulties persist, students may lose confidence, feel demoralized, and may even experience debilitating depression or anxiety.

When you think about all that is involved in conducting a dissertation study, it is easy to feel intimidated and daunted because it is such a large task that requires sustained effort over a long period of time. Most graduate students I have encountered tend to relate to their dissertation as one large entity. They wake up in the morning and think, "I need to work on my dissertation today." I have witnessed hundreds of doctoral students give themselves instructions such as "work on my dissertation" or "work all weekend" or something only slightly better such as "write literature review" or "write chapter 4." Instructions such as these are problematic for most students. They are almost equivalent to telling yourself to "do nothing" or "procrastinate all weekend and then if you are lucky complete 2 hours of work on Sunday night." Instructing yourself to "work on my dissertation" or "write my literature review" can be a bit like standing at the base of Mount Everest and saying, "Climb Mount Everest today." The task is too big, and you do not have a sense of what smaller steps you can take toward working your way up the dissertation mountain.

When you have large, ambiguously defined dissertation goals, you are more apt to feel overwhelmed and struggle to figure out where to begin and how to systematically tackle the work at hand. It is easy to procrastinate and delay your work because you are not sure how to get started. It is not clear how to direct your energy, and consequently much of your energy gets used up trying to figure out what to do instead of actually doing it. In chapters 4 and 5, you will learn how to use a structured, project management approach to turn Mount Dissertation into a series of much smaller hills that you can more reasonably and realistically climb.

There are many other potential roadblocks to successfully completing a dissertation. Graduate students may lack adequate support from their advisor or have a committee that is embroiled in conflict. Some students work full or part time, are raising a family, have come back to graduate school later in life after having another career, have a serious or chronic illness, or care for an aging parent or sick relative. Some students have mental health issues, physical or learning disabilities, or some other life circumstances that make completing a dissertation challenging. I have worked with many students who live in a different city, state, or even country from the university they attend. These students find it challenging to work on their dissertation from afar.

The Specter of Being All But Dissertation

Many graduate students admitted into doctoral programs never begin working on their dissertation, or, once they do, never finish the project. It is commonly stated that approximately 50% of all doctoral students do not complete their degrees (Council of Graduate Schools, 2004). Yet no longitudinal research covering a large number of institutions, disciplines, and students supports this notion. Some smaller scale studies examining cohorts of doctoral students across a variety of fields and limited numbers of universities indicate completion rates varying from a low of 33% for students in large doctoral programs in English, history, and political science (Bowen & Rudenstine, 1992) to a high of 76% for students in the biomedical and behavioral sciences supported by national training award grants from the National Institute of Health (Pion, 2001).

Bair and Haworth (1999) conducted a metasynthesis of 118 sources examining completion rates of doctoral students. The main overall trend they found is that attrition rates were lower in the laboratory sciences than in the social sciences and humanities. Precise attrition rates for particular fields are not available. According to Bowen and Rudenstine (1992), roughly 20% of students who are admitted to doctoral candidacy obtaining the "all but dissertation," or ABD, status do not complete their degree. Most of the students who exit doctoral programs do so before they reach the dissertation phase. For those who do reach the dissertation phase, having difficulty with the dissertation is positively correlated with student attrition (Bair & Haworth, 1999). Students leave doctoral programs before earning their degree for many reasons. Nonetheless, it is likely that concerns about successfully completing a dissertation contribute to doctoral-student attrition.

Some students may go on to better endeavors when they leave graduate school. Yet many students who exit school without their degree leave with a feeling of failure and regret. Also, they may limit their career potential and even their future earning power. When graduate students do not earn their doctoral degrees, they are not the only ones who suffer negative consequences. Universities invest money and other resources (most obviously faculty time) in graduate students, and it is a loss to these institutions when students use these resources but do not earn a doctoral degree (Diffley, 2005). As the pool of financial resources shrinks at many universities in the United States, the concern about attrition grows. In fact, many universities around the country have become increasingly concerned with the number of students who matriculate into doctoral programs but exit graduate school before earning a PhD. In recognition of the urgency to reduce attrition rates, some universities have begun to offer services such as dissertation workshops, access to editors and writing coaches, education for faculty on advising and mentoring students, dissertation support groups at counseling centers, and online resources, manuals, and guidelines designed to help graduate students with the dissertation process.

It is possible that like many students, you have responded to the inevitable challenges of such a huge project by becoming fearful of engaging fully in your dissertation work. You may be concerned that you will not be successful or will be viewed poorly in the eyes of others (faculty in particular). Thus, you may be losing the intellectual curiosity you had when you came to graduate school. The enthusiasm and excitement you had to learn may have been supplanted by negative thinking, emotional distress, and unproductive behaviors.

The Opportunity of a Doctoral Dissertation

No matter how difficult the dissertation path has been for you so far, there is hope. You can find a way to complete your dissertation and even enjoy the experience (okay, maybe you won't enjoy it all of the time, but you will at least some of the time). First, it is helpful to focus on your accomplishments so far in graduate school and with your dissertation. Most students tell me that it is far easier for them to think of dissertation disappointments than accomplishments. It is easy to overlook your dissertation accomplishments and achievements and lose sight of what is going well. For example, you may have successfully completed quite a few classes at this point in your graduate career, selected a topic you are genuinely interested in, or created an innovative way to study the questions you have posed. Yet it is often easier to find fault with yourself and your dissertation and berate yourself for procrastinating or for not being a better writer. However, a balanced perspective is much more productive.

When you examine your accomplishments, you can learn a great deal. Your accomplishments tell the story of your personal secrets of success and provide you with vital information about how to be successful as you complete your degree. Also, your disappointments provide invaluable lessons that can help you do things differently in the future (Ditzler, 1994). Rarely do students get the opportunity to step back and consider what important lessons there are to learn from the successes and challenges they face.

What follows is a series of exercises (see Exercises 1.1 and 1.2) adapted from Ditzler (1994) to help you identify key dissertation accomplishments and disappointments as well as the important lessons or guidelines you can learn from them.

Although the examples of guidelines in Exercise 1.1 might sound generic, they were all meaningful to the students who created them. Your task in Exercise 1.2 is to mine your own accomplishments and disappointments to craft personal dissertation guidelines on the basis of your lived experience. You will get more mileage out of your guidelines if you take the time to carefully craft them on the basis of your actual dissertation experience. That being said, you are welcome to use any from the list in Exercise 1.1 that are inspiring to you. Follow the four-step process in Exercise 1.2 to craft your own dissertation guidelines.

Once you have selected your three guidelines, I encourage you to type them and put a copy where you will see them regularly. Any time you need some inspiration or things are not going well with your dissertation, refer to these guidelines for help. If you face new challenges over time, be willing to create new guidelines that better fit your situation. When you overcome difficulties or have small successes in the future, take the time to create new guidelines on the basis of those experiences to foster continued success.

In addition to learning lessons from your past experience, it is also important to consider your values. Your values are the intangible qualities you deeply believe are important to demonstrate in your life. Values are not morals, statements about ethical behavior, or principles. Rather, they are the qualities that can help you live a fulfilled life (Whitworth, Kimsey-House, Kimsey-House, & Sandahl, 2007). Values are not something you possess or that you attain or that have an end point, like achieving a goal or an outcome (Hayes, Strosahl, & Wilson, 1999), but something you do or a quality of something you do. For example, if you value making a difference, your actions demonstrate making a difference. Making a difference is not done or attained just because you volunteer or tutor children for several months. Rather, the value represents an ongoing life direction. Although your values and goals are not the same, they are related (Eifert & Forsyth, 2005). Your values underlie many, if not all, of your goals.

Students often forget that they have important values, such as life-long learning, making a difference, creativity, innovation, collaboration,

EXERCISE 1.1

Identify Your Dissertation Accomplishments and Disappointments

In the space provided or on a separate piece of paper, write down your dissertation accomplishments and disappointments. If you are not yet at the dissertation phase, you can write down accomplishments and disappointments you have in graduate school more generally or regarding a specific project such as your master's thesis. Be as honest as possible, and write down everything you can think of regarding what has gone well and what has not.

My Dissertation Accomplishments:

Examples:
I have collected all of my data.
I was awarded a dissertation fellowship.
I am very proud of my proposal.
I have a great relationship with my advisor.

I regularly make time for my dissertation.
My research questions are important.
I have learned a great deal.
I have completed drafts of two chapters.

My Dissertation Disappointments:

Examples:
I still don't have a topic.
My advisor is very critical.
My committee is unsupportive.
I constantly doubt myself.

I waste so much time on the Internet.
I am struggling with statistics.
I let myself become very isolated.
I procrastinate too much.

(continued)

EXERCISE 1.1 (*Continued*)

After taking the time to list your accomplishments and disappointments, you are ready to learn important lessons from your past experience about how to be successful in the future. For example, you may be able to see that you need to challenge yourself to work when you feel unmotivated, that meeting regularly with your advisor leads to greater productivity, or that you need to make writing rough drafts and letting go of perfectionism a real priority. Perhaps you need to change your work environment or cut back on nondissertation activities for the next few months.

These lessons can be summarized as guidelines, short memorable phrases that start with a verb telling you what to do rather than what not to do (Ditzler, 1994). Below are some guidelines created by my clients based on this exercise.

Examples of Guidelines:

Honor my work.	Keep a clean, organized office.
Tolerate ambiguity.	Stick with it when the work gets tough.
Ask for help when I need it.	Let go of excessive standards.
Keep a positive attitude.	Be willing to make a mess.
Believe the work will get done.	Embrace the struggle.
Trust my instincts.	Enjoy challenges.
Believe in myself.	Know that tomorrow is another day.
Enjoy the process.	Take good care of myself.
Do the hard work first.	Seek support and encouragement.
Set positive intentions for work sessions.	Let my values show me the way.

Note. From *Your Best Year Yet!* (pp. 35–45; 47–59), by J. Ditzler, 1994, New York: Warner Books. Copyright 1994 by Grand Central Publishing. Adapted with permission.

EXERCISE 1.2

Create Your Own Dissertation Guidelines

Based on your lists of accomplishments and disappointments identified in Exercise 1.1, follow the four steps provided here to create your dissertation guidelines.

Step 1: Review your accomplishments and ask yourself the following questions. Write the answers below:

What has been the secret of my successes and accomplishments to date?
What worked well?
What has helped me be productive?
What would I like to see myself do again?
What strategies help me think, synthesize research or ideas, write, or develop a framework/argument/methodological approach?
How was I able to achieve what I did?

(continued)

EXERCISE 1.2 (*Continued*)

Step 2: Review your disappointments, and ask yourself the following questions. Write the answers below.

What did not work and why?

What would have worked better?

What lesson is there in each of my disappointments, failures, or mistakes?

What would I like to see myself do instead?

How could I work better?

What would help me procrastinate less and be more productive?

_____

_____

_____

_____

_____

_____

Step: 3: Create guidelines using the following three instructions. Look at the examples of guidelines for inspiration.

1. Start guidelines with a verb.
2. Create short, catchy, memorable phrases.
3. Say what you will do in positive terms (e.g., "Be positive" rather than "Don't be negative").

My Dissertation Guidelines:

_____   _____

_____   _____

_____   _____

_____   _____

_____   _____

_____   _____

_____   _____

_____   _____

As suggested by Ditzler (1994), it is a good idea to narrow down your list to three key guidelines. Ask yourself, of the guidelines I have listed, which three would make the biggest difference in improving both the process and product of my dissertation activities? Selecting these guidelines will help you focus on what is most important and increase the odds that you will remember and apply the guidelines in the future.

Step 4: Identify three key dissertation guidelines.

1. _____

2. _____

3. _____

Note. From *Your Best Year Yet!* (pp. 61–72), by J. Ditzler, 1994, New York: Warner Books. Copyright 1994 by Grand Central Publishing. Adapted with permission.

community, risk taking, and integrity. Values such as these can be important drivers or sources of motivation and inspiration in the world of academia and in the pursuit of a doctoral degree. Values can help guide your behavior when you face challenging or stressful times as you work on your dissertation. Also, being aware of your values helps remind you that other qualities and capacities besides intelligence are significant in life. In academic environments, being intelligent is often valued above and beyond other human qualities and capacities. Students end up believing that they need to prove they are smart enough, good enough, and worthy enough to earn a doctorate. Consequently, they may lose touch with values-driven goals and even their values themselves.

I know that you have important values in your life that inspire and motivate you. Many of these values play an important role in why you are seeking a doctoral degree. The experience of completing a dissertation can be an excellent opportunity for you to reconnect with your values and set the stage for a fulfilled postdoctoral life in which you aim to authentically express yourself, your values, and the gifts you have to offer. Ask yourself why you originally decided to pursue a PhD or why you stayed in graduate school despite the sacrifices you may have had to make. Then ask yourself what values completing your dissertation will allow you to demonstrate. These questions and those in the exercise that follows (adapted from Ditzler, 1994, and Whitworth et al., 2007) will help you to reconnect with your values. As you complete Exercise 1.3, I encourage you to reflect on the qualities that are most important to you rather than writing down what values you think you "should" have. Values are not right or wrong; they are just what you care about demonstrating in your life (Hayes & Smith, 2005).

EXERCISE 1.3

What Are My Values?

Use the following questions to identify your personal values, using the space provided to list them.
   What values do I want to demonstrate in my life?
   What values represent who I am?
   What impact do I want to have on others?
   What do I hope to achieve by earning a doctorate in my field?
   How will I impact the world around me by earning a doctorate?
   When I am at my best, what qualities are present?
   When I am moved or inspired, what qualities in myself or others are present?
   What do I want to be remembered for?
   What is the legacy I want to leave?

(continued)

EXERCISE 1.3 (*Continued*)

Examples:

Making a difference	Creativity
Contribution	Service
Collaboration	Flexibility
Excellence	Lifelong learning
Integrity	Freedom of self-expression

_____   _____

_____   _____

_____   _____

_____   _____

_____   _____

_____   _____

_____   _____

Type up your key values and keep this list with the guidelines you developed in the previous exercises. Together, they will become your personal north star, inspiring you and motivating you to hang in there during challenging times.

Looking Forward

My aim in writing this book is to help you find new ways of completing your dissertation that will not only help you earn your degree but also will enable you to get more out of the experience, both academically and personally. It is all too easy to become caught up in the former and lose sight of the latter. Although the skills, knowledge, and capabilities you learn in graduate school will be valuable, what you learn about yourself—your values, beliefs, emotions, behaviors—and what you can change for the better in that regard will be invaluable. In the next two chapters, you will learn how graduate students often get trapped in patterns of thinking, behavior, and emotions that interfere with their dissertation experience and how you can find your way through these challenging experiences.

The Traps of Negative Thinking, Feeling, and Behaving

2

T he work of a doctoral dissertation is clearly challenging. But it is not just the actual work that makes the road to a PhD so tough. Along the way, students are bound to experience thinking, feeling, and behaving challenges that make the dissertation journey more difficult. It is near impossible, I believe, to earn a PhD without having negative beliefs, emotions, or behavior at some point. In fact, you can expect to encounter these roadblocks on your path to a doctoral degree. If you think you are the only student in your department experiencing negative thoughts, feelings, or behavior associated with doing your dissertation, I am 100% certain you are incorrect.

As a dissertation coach, I often wish I could somehow take my clients on a tour of the internal world of other graduate students. My aim would be to show them that self-doubt, anxiety, fear, procrastination, perfectionism, and other unpleasant unwanted experiences are not unique to them. Your private experience—how you think, feel, and behave in relationship to your dissertation—is more similar to that of other students than it is different. I realize that my last statement may be hard to believe. Doing a dissertation can be a very isolating experience in which you have little contact with other students by the time you reach this phase of graduate school. Even if you do have such contact, other students may not be very forthcoming about their own private dissertation experience.

One of the cruelest aspects of doing a dissertation is that in the academic world there is rarely a candid dialogue about just how common it is to have negative, self-doubting beliefs and thoughts, unpleasant emotions, and self-defeating behavior. Believe me when I say that you are not alone in your dissertation experience, no matter how confident, organized, competent, or productive your peers may seem. To be a doctoral student is to experience the traps of negative thinking, feeling, and behaving at some point or many points on the dissertation journey. It is true that some people struggle more than others. If you have struggled a lot (or a little), this chapter and chapter 3 are written for you.

In this chapter, I show you how to recognize the common thinking, feeling, and behaving traps that can so easily ensnare you as you work on your dissertation. Chapter 3 will help you find your way out of these traps.

Thinking Traps

Negative thinking is remarkably common among doctoral students. Yet many students remain unaware of the power this kind of negative thinking has on their ability to maintain motivation, be productive, and carry out the day-to-day activities of a dissertation study. It is important to recognize that the way you think and how you respond to these thoughts can have a direct impact on how you feel and behave in connection with your dissertation. When your perceptions or thoughts are negative, they can lead to a downward spiral of negative emotions, behavior, and more negative thoughts that continually reinforce each other.

POSITIVE THINKING

Before I go deeper in the discussion of thinking traps, it is important to acknowledge that you may well have lots of positive beliefs and thoughts about yourself and the process of completing a dissertation. Academia may be an environment in which you thrive and feel inspired. I want to be clear that I do not believe that all graduate students seriously struggle with negative, limiting beliefs, nor do I believe that students who experience limiting beliefs struggle with those beliefs all of the time. Yet I do know that the typical graduate student I encounter (albeit a biased sample of students who attend dissertation workshops, coaching groups, and seek individual dissertation coaching) experience some degree of negative thinking that has an impact on their self-confidence, productivity, work output, and overall experience of completing a dissertation.

TYPICAL NEGATIVE THINKING

Often when I lead a dissertation workshop at a university, I hand out notepaper to every student in the audience. I ask each of them to write down the most common negative thoughts they have about their dissertation or their own ability to finish this project. After they have recorded their negative thoughts, I collect the notepaper and read the results of the group exercise aloud. The messages in the pile of notepaper I receive, no matter the prestige of a student's university or field of study, are virtually interchangeable from one workshop to another. Exhibit 2.1 is a list of many of the negative and self-defeating thoughts identified by students in my dissertation workshops.

EXHIBIT 2.1

Common Negative and Self-Defeating Thoughts Among Doctoral Students

---

Thoughts about academic skills and abilities

"They made a mistake admitting me in this program."

"I will never be able to come up with an original thesis."

"My writing skills are not at the level they need to be."

"I am just not capable of finishing."

"I am not an original thinker."

"I lack the knowledge base a person should have to deserve a doctorate."

"I do not understand statistics well enough to carry out a dissertation study."

"I think there must be something wrong with me. No matter how hard I try to organize my thoughts, I can't seem to figure out how to conceptualize my dissertation study."

"I am terrible at public speaking. I do not know how I will ever give a presentation at my dissertation defense."

"English is not my first language, which makes doing a good dissertation impossible."

"I am not sure I can clearly convey my topic or my ideas."

Thoughts about intelligence

"I am not as smart as people think I am. I'll be found out as a fraud eventually."

"I am not smart, I just work hard."

"I am just good at tricking people into thinking I am smart."

"Other students seem so intelligent and organized. I don't measure up."

"I am afraid I am not smart enough to earn a PhD."

"Because I struggle with statistics, I constantly question my intelligence and abilities."

Thoughts about fear of failure

"I have a proposal written, but I am terrified to defend it before my committee. I am afraid they will tell me it is unacceptable and that I will be asked to leave the program."

"What if I fail my dissertation defense? What would my friends and family think?"

"I have several chapters written, but I am scared to give them to my advisor for feedback. What if he rips my work to shreds and tells me my work is insufficient to earn a PhD."

"When I finish my degree, then I will have to get a job. What if no one will hire me?"

(continued)

EXHIBIT 2.1 (*Continued*)

Perfectionist thoughts

"My dissertation must be perfect."

"It has taken me so long to get my dissertation done so now I feel that it has to be incredible. Otherwise, my committee will wonder what I have been doing all this time."

"I can't seem to stop obsessing about my writing. I think I need to turn in work that is of outstanding quality even when it is a first draft."

"I am so worried about what other people think of me in my department. I want to be a 'perfect student' in the eyes of faculty members."

Thoughts about one's behavior, life circumstances, and character

"I am too lazy and unmotivated to ever finish a dissertation."

"I am taking too long. My topic will have been done by someone else by the time I finish."

"I started graduate school too late in life. I am too old to earn a PhD."

"I procrastinate too much and no matter what I do I can't seem to do what I promise I will do."

"I feel so burned out at this point. In my lifetime, I've been in school for over 20 years, and I wonder everyday if I have the stamina to finish my dissertation."

"Between my job, family, and graduate work, I'll never have the time I need to finish my dissertation."

"I always get my research/teaching assistant work done on time. Why can't I get my own dissertation work that matters done? I am only motivated to do work for others."

"I can't get myself to do any meaningful work unless I have an entire day to work."

Thoughts about faculty members and relationships with them

"I haven't talked to my chairperson in so long that I am afraid to call or e-mail her for fear she will tell me to get a new chairperson."

"My advisor gives other students more attention. I am not sure she believes I can finish."

"My committee is so unsupportive. None of them have contacted me in 6 months."

"My advisor does not take the responsibility of advising students seriously enough."

"My advisor is so critical that I am reluctant to give him the latest version of my dissertation."

What is your reaction when you read this list of thoughts? When I lead dissertation workshops, many students report feeling relieved to discover that other students experience similar doubts, worries, and concerns. My hope in doing this exercise is that students will experience some liberation. So often students believe that the mere existence of negative thoughts is verification that the thoughts are true. "Why else would I have negative, self-doubting thoughts if they were not true?" you may wonder. Hearing a large group of doctoral students express their negative thoughts in such a candid way often helps students recognize that their private experience of doing a dissertation is more similar to than different from that of their peers. They are able to consider that the presence of negative thoughts is not proof that they are true.

When you read the list of thoughts in Exhibit 2.1, it is clear that these thoughts are negative. They are thoughts that are full of self-doubt, angst, and fear. But luckily many psychologists, including Albert Ellis,

Carol Dweck, and Steven Hayes, have spent considerable time examining how people get caught in the trap of negative thinking. In this chapter, I discuss four key thinking traps and how they may be adversely affecting your dissertation progress. First, I hope to help you understand where negative thinking comes from and how it is perpetuated in our minds.

UNDERSTANDING NEGATIVE THINKING

So where does all of this negative thinking come from? Your mind is designed by evolution to help you survive. Consequently, the mind constantly and without conscious awareness categorizes present events and explains, predicts, compares, and judges those events (Hayes & Smith, 2005). As human beings interact with the world and other people, they develop beliefs that help them to organize and understand their experience in a coherent, organized manner (J. Beck, 1995). The beliefs that are central to how humans view themselves and the world in which they live are considered *core beliefs*. Core beliefs are beliefs that are so fundamental that human beings accept them as absolute truths. Virtually all human beings have at least some core beliefs that are negative. For example, some people have the belief that they are incompetent, weak, powerless, out of control, ineffective, or unlovable (J. Beck, 1995). Core beliefs such as these leave humans vulnerable to interpreting the situations they encounter in their lives in a negative way.

Beliefs are enduring cognitions that you are generally unaware of. As we go through life and encounter various situations, we are constantly and automatically interpreting our experiences through the lens of our core beliefs. These interpretations are commonly referred to as automatic thoughts because they seem to spring up automatically as you interpret the various situations you encounter in your life. The core beliefs you have will influence how you construe different situations. For example, if you have a core belief that you are intellectually inferior, then you are likely to have automatic thoughts about receiving a low score on an exam such as, "I am never going to pass this class"; "If I can't do well on a test, then I'll never make it to the dissertation phase"; or "I am such a loser." If you are asked to reconceptualize your dissertation proposal by your advisor, you might have thoughts such as "I'll never be able to understand the revisions my advisor wants me to make" or "I'll be humiliated at my defense meeting." You are more likely to be aware of the automatic cognitions than core beliefs (Mullin, 2000). Identifying automatic thoughts can be a good first step to determine what deeper core beliefs are having an impact on your dissertation experience.

It is important to understand that core beliefs are not necessarily active at all times. For example, if a student believes, "I am not smart enough," then that belief is not necessarily activated unless the student is in a situation in which he or she is struggling with an intellectual task or his or her academic work is questioned or challenged by a person of authority. When the belief is activated, the student is likely to perceive the event that is transpiring through the lens of the core belief "I am not smart enough." If a faculty member questions the student's dissertation data-analysis strategy, the student may interpret the event as a clear validation of his belief that he is not smart enough. Another student who does not share this belief may interpret the situation differently and believe that being questioned is a valuable part of learning and developing a sound study. Our core beliefs and the thoughts that follow them are important in shaping our perceptions of our experiences and ourselves.

THE SELF-REINFORCING NATURE OF THOUGHTS

Our core beliefs and automatic thoughts tend to perpetuate themselves. People generally seek information to support their assumptions, interpretations, and thoughts. Human beings tend to pay more attention to events that confirm their beliefs than those that contradict their beliefs (J. Beck, 1995). This tendency can create problems. For example, if you believe a faculty member in your program does not like you, then you are more likely to pay close attention to how the faculty member interacts with you as you look for any indication of disapproval. You may take it personally when he or she asks you tough questions about your research, cancels a meeting with you, or walks by you in the hallway without saying hello. Your belief acts as a filter through which you interpret your experience influencing your perceptions, what you notice, what you do not notice, and what you remember. Therefore, you are more likely to perceive information that seems to confirm your belief that you are not liked and ignore evidence that contradicts your belief. In addition, your core beliefs can influence how you interact with the world in a way that actually changes your environment and important outcomes in your life. For example, if you believe you are incompetent, then you may withhold effective action toward dissertation tasks and thus perform poorly on those tasks and view your poor performance as evidence of your incompetence. In this way, your core belief becomes a self-fulfilling prophecy (Mullin, 2000).

THINKING TRAP 1: THINKING ERRORS

The first thinking trap is the tendency of human beings to have erroneous beliefs about the adversity and challenges they face. Albert Ellis (e.g., Ellis, 1994, 2001; Ellis & Dryden, 1990; Ellis & MacLaren, 1998) detailed what these beliefs are and how they cause negative and disturbing emotions and self-defeating behavior. Ellis developed a method of psychotherapy called rational emotive behavior therapy, which focuses on recognizing and changing thoughts, feelings, and behavior and being more accepting of oneself. Although other cognitive therapies may be considered more current in the field of psychotherapy, I have found Ellis's approach very useful as I coach graduate students to finish their dissertations. Ellis (2001) indicated that human beings have many different negative beliefs but there are three dominant and universal types that contribute to negative thoughts, negative emotions, and self-defeating behavior.

Negative Belief 1: Excessive Demands

The first type of negative belief is the tendency of human beings to have excessive standards or demands (Ellis, 2001; Ellis & MacLaren, 1998). These excessive standards or demands can be applied to (a) the self (e.g., "I should not struggle when I write" or "I absolutely must be motivated to work on my dissertation"), (b) other people (e.g., "My advisor must not criticize my work"), and (c) how the dissertation process works in general (e.g., "The dissertation process is so hard—it should not be this way"). Having an excessive standard or demand is an irrational belief that involves rigid, absolute thinking about how you, others, and the world *should* or *must* be. Graduate students often believe that they must under all conditions do important tasks well and be approved of by significant others, or else they deem themselves inadequate, unworthy, or unacceptable in some way.

Many of the negative thoughts written on notepaper during my workshops are excessive demands. For example, students frequently write down some version of the statement, "I am not smart enough to earn a PhD." What these students are really saying is "I should be/I must be smarter if I want to earn a PhD." When I first work with clients as their dissertation coach, I often uncover many rigid, absolute beliefs that they have about their ability to execute a dissertation study such as, "I should be able to write my literature review in a week," "I should have been finished by now," or "I must be able to write perfectly or I'll be seen as incompetent." These thoughts may seem obviously irrational when you read them. Yet such awareness does not make you immune to having thoughts such as these, especially when you are under stress.

It is quite normal and even advantageous to have strong preferences, goals, and desires such as "I want to develop a great dissertation study that will help me land an academic job." Nothing is wrong with striving for excellence, success, approval, or comfort. However, problems arise when your preferences, goals, and desires become absolute demands. If you raise your preferences to the level of absolute demands of how you and the conditions around you have to be, you are basically telling yourself that anything less than what meets your demands is unacceptable (Ellis, 2001).

When your expectations of yourself and your dissertation experience become absolute demands, you become vulnerable to negative emotions and self-defeating behavior. If you believe, for example, that you absolutely must not be required to make revisions after your defense because needing to do so would be a sign of your inadequacy, you are likely to feel upset, even depressed and demoralized if you do indeed need to make them. You may feel angry with your committee for making it impossible for you to live up to your own demands. As a result, you may delay making the revisions because facing them makes you feel inadequate, anxious, angry, or depressed. Consider the following alternative way of preferring instead of demanding in this situation:

> I would prefer that my committee not require me to make revisions after my dissertation defense, and I recognize that it is quite common for students to be asked to make changes post-defense. If it happens to me, I may feel uncomfortable and even inadequate. But such feelings do not have to stop me from working. I can have those feelings and make the revisions anyway. Also, being asked to make revisions will improve my dissertation and likely make it easier to publish my research.

This alternative way of thinking about being required to make revisions is more flexible and accepting. Imagine how you would feel if you believed this statement of preference and how you would respond to being required to make revisions to your dissertation. I would guess you would be much better able to handle the experience and take proactive action to amend your dissertation after your defense.

Suggesting that you become aware of excessive demands and prefer when possible does not mean that I am suggesting you abandon your standards outright. Obviously, it is important to work hard in graduate school and strive to learn and succeed academically. It is also reasonable to have strong preferences and high standards for your academic work. Yet if you develop rigid, unrealistic demands of yourself and others, you are likely to continue thinking in negative ways and experience negative emotions and self-defeating behavior. Unfortunately, many students fail to recognize that they have developed excessive standards and demands. They simply believe that their standards and demands must be met. They remain unaware that thinking in a more flexible way is even possible. Having preferences for success and high performance gives you room to be human and will likely help you better enjoy the experience of conducting a dissertation and being a doctoral student.

Why are graduate students so prone to absolute demands and excessive standards? There are several reasons. First, graduate school is a setting where students' performance and intellectual abilities are frequently evaluated. The evaluations are primarily about their academic performance, which students often view as a global evaluation of their intelligence, worthiness to attain a doctoral degree, and possibly even their worth as a human being. Thus, students are likely to be fearful of being criticized, evaluated as performing poorly, or failing to meet the standards required to earn a PhD. Second, students have invested a great deal of energy, time, and money before reaching the dissertation phase of graduate school. From a student's point of view, the stakes are very high when it comes to doing a dissertation. If you are not successful, all of the years of hard work and financial sacrifice will not result in earning your long-sought-after degree. Failure comes to be viewed as an outcome that absolutely must be avoided. It becomes quite normal to demand of yourself, "I must not fail. I must earn my degree"; "I must write perfectly to succeed"; or "I should be working harder and faster." Demanding that you absolutely must perform a certain way gives you the perception that your risk of failure is lower. In actuality, excessive demands can increase the likelihood of failure, as rigid demands often lead to unhealthy emotions such as anxiety and self-defeating behavior such as procrastination.

Third, graduate school is a time when students are indoctrinated into a set of beliefs about academia and academic performance. Some of these beliefs are quite reasonable and may actually be based on written department guidelines or graduate student handbooks. Such beliefs include, "Students must demonstrate that they are able to carry out a sound dissertation study as the final step toward earning a PhD"; "Faculty and students must use ethical standards when it comes to conducting research"; and "Plagiarism is not acceptable and is justification for dismissal from the doctoral program."

Other beliefs are not found in a student or department handbook but from the student's perspective often seem to be true. This set of beliefs includes many myths about what it means to be a successful student and academic, for example, "I must have mastery of statistics to earn a PhD"; "My advisor is able to write a literature review in a weekend. I should be able to do the same"; or "My dissertation is critical to my future career and what I'll do the rest of my life. I must write an incredible dissertation."

It is true you need to perform well and meet high standards in graduate school. Yet I caution you against inflating these demands so that they become rigid and excessive. For example, it is true that you need to be able to work independently to earn a PhD. But is working independently the same as never asking for help and believing that you need to figure out everything yourself? You need to be able to write in a way that is clear, cogent, and accurate. But is that the same as writing a perfect draft the first time you sit down to write a chapter? Be careful about demanding that you live up to standards that have more to do with academic mythology than the reality of what it means to be successful. Exercise 2.1 gives you the opportunity to identify some of your own rigid, dogmatic thinking (e.g., should, must, have to).

EXERCISE 2.1

Identify Excessive Demands

Write down any excessive demands you may have, including rigid beliefs about how you, others, or the world around you should or must be (e.g., I should be able to write faster; I should be smarter; My advisor should be more available to me):

_____

_____

_____

_____

Negative Belief 2: "Awfulizing" and Low-Frustration Tolerance

The natural outcome of having excessive demands and standards is that human beings tend to anticipate that experiencing adversity or failing to meet these demands and standards would be awful, even devastating. Ellis (2001) coined a term for this type of negative thinking: *awfulizing*. If you believe you should be smarter, for example, you are likely to believe that it is awful or terrible that you are not as smart as you think you should be. The fear of experiencing something awful reinforces the demand that an adverse event absolutely must not occur. For example, when students contemplate receiving feedback on their dissertation work, they may tell themselves that it would be terrible to receive critical feedback without really thinking through what would in fact be so terrible about it. As they believe that it will be awful, even devastating, to receive critical feedback, they then demand even more intensely that this situation must not occur. When such a demand is present, the student is likely to become fearful of criticism and perhaps go to great lengths to avoid such an outcome.

Common ways I have seen graduate students awfulize are when they have beliefs such as, "Waiting so long for feedback is terrible"; "If I fail my dissertation defense, I would be devastated"; "It is terrible that I struggle so much with statistics"; or "It is awful that I was not more productive last week." The alternative to awfulizing is recognizing that failing to meet your demands (which are unreasonable to begin with) is inconvenient, unpleasant, uncomfortable, or annoying—not awful, terrible, or devastating. If you can make such a cognitive shift, then you will be better able to relax rigid demands and stay engaged when difficulties with your dissertation arise. For example, a student who reminds himself that it is inconvenient and annoying (not awful and terrible) to wait a long time for feedback from his advisor is more likely to keep his anger in check and be able to diplomatically assert his need to receive feedback.

Related to the tendency to awfulize, human beings often believe that adversity or failing to meeting their demands is intolerable (Ellis & MacLaren, 1998). For example, students may believe that they should be able to write a first draft of a literature review easily without too much struggle. When these students do in fact struggle, they may tell themselves that they cannot tolerate writing when the writing is not easy. Ellis (2001) termed this type of irrational thinking *low-frustration tolerance,* or LFT. This means having little or no tolerance for adversity in life and the reality that our demands cannot always be met. Often students believe that they absolutely must not experience adversity. They believe that conditions must be the way they want them to be and tell themselves that it is unbearable when they are not. A person who believes that adversity is intolerable is less likely to focus on proactive action they can take and more likely to remain entrenched in their belief that the situation is indeed intolerable (Ellis & MacLaren, 1998).

Students also frequently have LFT for the typical challenges, difficulties, and mundane aspects of dissertation work. In truth, doing dissertation work is often tough and seems to exceed our abilities. It involves unpleasant or challenging conversations with faculty, issues collecting and analyzing data, and difficulty writing. At other times, the actual work of doing a dissertation is downright tedious and boring. According to Knaus (2002), LFT is the most common cause of procrastination. When you think a particular task is intolerable in some way, you usually believe you will not be able to handle the frustration of completing the task and sidetrack yourself. The next time you notice yourself thinking, "I can't do this now," or "This task is too boring/tedious/bothersome/hard," there is a very good chance LFT is at play. Once LFT beliefs are activated, it is easy to focus on the feelings of frustration, boredom, and distress they cause. The feelings then tend to become magnified and procrastination ensues as you seek to avoid the dissertation tasks you perceive as difficult, unpleasant, or intolerable (Knaus, 2002).

The reality of doing a dissertation does not always match your expectation of how you think the project should proceed or how you should perform. In response to this mismatch between expectations and reality, graduate students are vulnerable to awfulizing and experiencing LFT. Students then might have thoughts such as "Writing a literature review is awful," "I can't stand entering data," "This is so boring," "I hate working on my dissertation," or "I do not feel like working." Following such thoughts students may think "I can do this work later" or "I will wait to work until I feel more motivated," which fuels the behavior of avoiding dissertation work. Students are usually unaware of how the tendency to awfulize and having LFT interferes with their productivity. Exercise 2.2 offers you the opportunity to identify these tendencies regarding your dissertation.

EXERCISE 2.2

Identify Awfulizing and Low-Frustration Tolerance

Write down any beliefs you have about how failing to meet your demands or carrying out a dissertation study is awful, terrible, or intolerable (e.g., It is awful that I can't write faster; I can't stand entering data):

_____

_____

_____

_____

Negative Belief 3: Overgeneralizing (The Disco Ball Error)

The third negative belief is the tendency to overgeneralize and damn oneself or others. This type of belief occurs when we label ourselves or others or even the dissertation process itself in global ways instead of labeling specific behavior or aspects of the dissertation process (Ellis, 2001; Ellis & MacLaren, 1998). For example, if your advisor tells you to make some substantial revisions to your dissertation, you may label yourself as "not smart enough" or overgeneralize and tell yourself "I will never finish." Overgeneralizing occurs when you make a global evaluation about yourself, others, or a situation on the basis of one or a few events, situations, or experiences.

Fundamentally, when you overgeneralize you are failing to maintain a pluralistic point of view. By this, I mean seeing yourself, others, and the world in which you live as complex and multifaceted. Let me give you a visual illustration of my point: Imagine a disco ball. What covers the exterior of a disco ball? Hundreds, maybe thousands of small, square mirrors depending on the size of the ball. Imagine I have a disco ball that represents you. Each individual mirror on the exterior of that disco ball represents some aspect of who you are in all of your complexity. There would be mirrors that represent your strengths, abilities, talents, weaknesses, values, the rich landscape of your intellectual capacity, your instincts, how you respond to opportunities and challenges, how you gather and store information, your coping style, what motivates you, your temperament, emotional patterns, habits, how your family of origin and childhood experiences have affected you, all the different aspects of your personality, and everything else that is you.

Now, imagine a situation in which you received some negative feedback from your advisor or you were unsuccessful in your latest effort to analyze your data. Maybe you had a day where you procrastinated all day. Imagine that the negative incident is one mirror on the larger disco ball that is you. What we tend to do in situations such as these is evaluate ourselves as if all of who we are is based only on that one incident, that one mirror on the disco ball. It is as if some critical feedback, a failed experiment, or a day of procrastination represents the entire disco ball. When you overgeneralize and damn yourself, or make the "disco ball error," you evaluate and label yourself in negative ways that are inaccurate, unfair, and that fail to recognize all of who you are. You become unable to maintain a pluralistic point of view where you see yourself, others, or situations as complex and multifaceted. It is also easy to make the disco ball error about other people. For example, if your advisor is especially critical you may damn him as a "jerk." In reality, he may have given you critical feedback (his behavior), but it is an overgeneralization to evaluate and categorize him globally on the basis of his behavior.

When you overgeneralize, you risk confusing your worth as a human being with your performance, assuming that poor performance makes you bad, unworthy, or inadequate. Similarly, when you succeed, receive praise, or perform well, you are apt to conclude that you are a good, intelligent, and worthy person (Ellis, 2001). Either set of assumptions leaves you vulnerable to evaluating your worth on the basis of your own or others' evaluation of your performance. Striving to maintain a pluralistic point of view will help you develop a rich and nuanced understanding of yourself and the world around you. You will be better able to consider multiple interpretations of a given situation and be flexible in your view of yourself, others, and the world in which you live. Most important, you will be better able to see yourself as a person of worth regardless of your performance.

At the age of 14, I made the disco ball error in a way that had a huge impact on my life. I went to a competitive public high school outside of Philadelphia with many high-achieving students. As a sophomore, I, along with my fellow classmates took the PSAT, a practice version of the Scholastic Aptitude Test (SAT). Some time after taking the exam, we received our scores in our homeroom classrooms. At the time I took the exam you received a verbal score, a math score, and total score for both verbal and math combined.

I was dumbfounded and shocked when I saw that my score was well below what I expected. Quickly, I tried to make sense of what was happening. First, I thought there must be some mistake. As I stared at the numbers on the page, my heart sank and I struggled not to burst into tears. To my horror, my classmates began disclosing PSAT scores, and it seemed to me that everyone had received a higher score than I did. I responded by lying and telling people that I received a higher score. I was particularly dismayed to learn that students who seemed to struggle academically or who I considered to be less intelligent than I was had received higher scores than I did.

Later that day, I thought to myself, "How could I get such a low score? I thought I was smart. Other people tell me that I am smart. I get good grades. My teachers and peers consider me intelligent." As I tried to make sense of my PSAT score, I thought to myself, "I guess you are not actually that smart—I guess you are not as smart as other people think you are." I then began thinking about how I had studied hard to obtain high test scores in classes and how hard I had to work to succeed in math and geometry. I recalled how I memorized my oral presentations for social studies classes before delivering them and thought about all the time I spent studying for chemistry exams. In light of my PSAT score, I determined that I was not actually smart. Rather, I concluded that I was able to trick people into thinking I was smart through the use of good verbal skills and hard work. In effect, I rewrote my academic history through the lens of the belief "I am not smart enough. I just work hard."

From that point on, every time I succeeded at an academic task I wondered whether my success was due to hard work and my skill at feigning intelligence. Any time I struggled, I thought back to my PSAT score and worried about its meaning and whether I really was intellectually inferior. I felt compelled to work very hard to prove myself and maintain the illusion that I was indeed intelligent. When I struggled academically, I accumulated more evidence of my intellectual inferiority. I went on to take the real SAT and received a much higher score, but because I studied for the test, I believed that my preparation invalidated the meaning of the better score. In my mind, I was still intellectually inferior. No matter what I accomplished, I was haunted by my PSAT score with the belief "I am not smart enough. I just work hard" echoing in my head in all of my academic pursuits.

My story is an illustration of overgeneralizing in an extreme way. On the basis of one score on a test that I took with zero preparation at age 14, I concluded that I was not smart. I made the disco ball error by concluding that one mirror on the larger disco ball—my PSAT score—was representative of my entire intellectual capacity. During graduate school, I began to recognize how this error had left me feeling inadequate, believing I was unintelligent, and always being on guard for fear that I would be exposed as incompetent. As a result of overgeneralizing, I became prone to having excessive demands (e.g., "I must prove I am smart," "I must have something intelligent to say in class so that I can ensure that people see me as intelligent"), and I believed that failing to meet my demands would be awful.

These ways of thinking all led me down a troubled road of feeling anxious, stressed, and even depressed at times. In addition, I developed many self-defeating behaviors, such as putting off work until the night before it was due and failing to complete many reading assignments (because it was so uncomfortable to do academic work that triggered my self-doubting beliefs). The consequences of my negative thinking were painful and reinforced my belief that I was not as intelligent as I "should" be.

Over time, as I recognized the error of my overgeneralized belief, I developed a more flexible view of my intellectual capacity. Today, I am confident that I am an intelligent woman with many skills and capacities. At the same time I am comfortable knowing that my intellectual capacity is rich and complex. I am intellectually strong in some areas and not in others. I also recognize that I am more capable of learning when I am less fearful of being intellectually inadequate. Thinking about myself as a complex, multifaceted person prevents me from seeing my intelligence in a black-or-white manner as if I am smart or not smart. Developing a more flexible view of my intellectual abilities has also helped me to recognize that there are many other aspects of myself, such as making a difference and being kind, that I value. Exercise 2.3 offers you the opportunity to identify how you have overgeneralized and made the disco ball error.

Other Common Thinking Errors

Psychologists have identified many types of beliefs and thoughts that interfere with people's lives. So far I have focused on excessive demands, awfulizing and LFT, and overgeneralizing. There are many variations and derivatives of these beliefs (Ellis & MacLaren, 1998). Below are some examples of other types of distorted thinking patterns. This is by no means an exhaustive list (see Antony & Swinson, 1998; A. T. Beck, 1976; and Burns, 1980, for more comprehensive lists of cognitive distortions). Rather, I am aiming to point out a few types of distorted thinking patterns that I often see among doctoral students.

All-or-Nothing Thinking

All-or-nothing thinking, also known as black-or-white thinking, is the tendency to see things as all good or all bad or all right and all wrong (Burns, 1980). People who make this error usually fail to see the gray area in between the extremes of all or nothing. This thinking error is related

---

EXERCISE 2.3

Identify Overgeneralizations

Write down any overgeneralizations you have made about yourself, others, or the world around you (e.g., I am not good at statistics; I have spent so many years procrastinating; I will never finish my dissertation; My advisor is a terrible mentor):

_____

_____

_____

_____

to making excessive demands for how things should be and overgeneralizing. Among doctoral students all-or-nothing thinking often sounds like, "I am struggling to organize my literature review. I'll never get this chapter done"; "Anything less than perfect on an exam is not good enough"; or "If I do not have all day to work, I can't get anything done."

Probability Overestimation

Human beings tend to make predictions about what will happen in their lives. Many people spend a lot of time anticipating outcomes for fear that conditions they desire will not be met (Ellis, 2001). When people make a probability overestimation, they are overestimating the likelihood that negative events will occur (Antony & Swinson, 1998). For example, a student may overestimate the likelihood that he will fail his dissertation defense or be unable to obtain human-subjects approval from the Institutional Review Board. Following this thinking error, the student is likely to engage in catastrophic thinking.

Catastrophic Thinking

In addition to making predictions about what will happen in their lives, people also make predictions about how they will handle what occurs. Catastrophic thinking involves two main types of cognitive distortions: (a) people incorrectly predict that a negative event would be unmanageable, awful, terrible, or devastating in some way; and (b) they incorrectly assume that they could not cope or handle the negative event if it indeed occurred (Antony & Swinson, 1998). If students overestimate the likelihood of a challenging dissertation defense, for example, they are also likely to overestimate how bad it would be and underestimate their capacity to handle such an event.

Focusing on the Negative

Once people are thinking negatively, they are more likely to focus on the negative aspects of events and disqualify the positive. It is as if they can only see the negative and filter out the positive aspects of a situation (Burns, 1980). For example, after a good meeting with an advisor, a graduate student disqualifies the meeting as a success because the last meeting was tense and difficult. This student thinks, "My meeting today seemed to go well, but the last meeting was so difficult that I am sure my advisor still thinks poorly of me."

THINKING TRAP 2: YOUR THEORY OF INTELLIGENCE

In addition to the trap of thinking errors identified by Ellis and other psychologists, there is a very important belief about intelligence that may have a significant impact on your dissertation experience. Until I conducted the research for this book, I was unaware of one of the most critical beliefs that impacts academic achievement, motivation, and satisfaction. This belief, when you understand it, has the potential to transform how you view yourself as a doctoral student and even more broadly as an intellectual being. The work of psychologist Carol Dweck demonstrated that whether students believe their intelligence is malleable or fixed has a profound impact on their academic performance, response to failure and challenges, and motivation. Most of us have never stopped and considered what we believe about human intelligence. We may believe we are smart or fear we are not smart enough, but rarely do we consider whether we believe we can cultivate our intelligence through effort.

Dweck and her colleagues (e.g., Dweck, 1990, 2000, 2006; Dweck & Leggett, 1988; Elliot & Dweck, 1988) demonstrated that students tend to have two distinct reactions to failure and two corresponding beliefs about intelligence. Although these research findings are based on students in elementary, junior high school, high school, and college, I believe the findings have direct implications for doctoral education. The results of this body of research indicate that changing what you believe about intelligence can impact your motivation to learn, how you respond to academic challenges, and your actual academic performance.

The two distinct reactions to failure described by Dweck (2000) are called the *helpless-oriented* and *mastery-oriented* patterns. Students with a helpless-oriented pattern view failure as something that is out of their control and think that nothing can be done to improve the situation. They tend to denigrate their intelligence, lose hope that they will succeed in the future, and experience negative emotions about their failures and abilities. Also, they are less likely to persist when they experience academic or intellectual challenges or deteriorating performance.

In contrast, students with the mastery-oriented pattern love learning, seek challenges, and persist in the face of obstacles. When they experience failure they do not blame anyone or anything. They do not even consider themselves to be failing. They know that they are experiencing difficulty, but unlike helpless-oriented students, they begin instructing and monitoring themselves to determine how they can improve their performance. For example, when faced with academic challenges, they give themselves self-motivating instructions such as "the harder it gets, the harder I should try" or "I should slow down and figure this out" (Dweck, 2000, p. 9). Mastery-oriented students enjoy challenges and view mistakes as opportunities for learning and growth. They are also more likely to have better academic performance because they see challenges as avenues to learn and develop new and more sophisticated strategies to meet and overcome those challenges. Helpless-oriented students, in contrast, view their intelligence and even their self-worth as being on the line when they are faced with academic difficulties. The critical difference between these two groups is that the mastery-oriented students do not see failure "as an indictment of themselves" (Dweck, 2000, p. 9) so the risk of seeking to meet intellectual challenges is not so great.

What causes students to have such different orientations to academic challenges? Research by Elliot and Dweck (1988) indicated that the goals of a student in achievement situations can directly create either a helpless- or a mastery-oriented response. Students with a helpless orientation tend to have performance goals that are about measuring ability. Such students are concerned about looking smart to others and themselves. In contrast, students with a mastery orientation are more likely to have learning goals that are about mastering new things. Students with learning goals aim to increase their competence, learn new skills, master new tasks, understand new things, and become smarter. Both types of goals are valid and natural to human beings. The danger is that when students overemphasize performance over learning goals, they are more likely to miss out on important and valuable learning opportunities and develop a helpless orientation (Dweck, 2000).

The particular orientation of a student to failure and their corresponding learning goals grow out of the way they understand intelligence. According to Dweck (2000), people understand intelligence in two ways. First, there is the entity theory, in which intelligence is viewed as a fixed trait that dwells within us and is unchangeable. Dweck (2006) referred to this belief as having a *fixed mind-set* about intelligence. Second, there is the incremental theory, in which intelligence is viewed as malleable and as something that can be cultivated through learning and increased through effort. Dweck (2006) referred to this belief as having a *growth mind-set* about intelligence. People with a fixed mind-set tend to worry about how much intelligence they have and become focused on determining if they have enough. They expend a lot of energy making sure they look smart and believe it is very important to avoid being seen as unintelligent. Overall, people with a fixed mind-set feel smart when they experience easy, low-effort successes and outperform others. They begin to doubt their intelligence when they need to exert effort and experience difficulty, setbacks, or outperforming peers. Thus, their self-esteem is threatened by intellectual challenges, and they are much more likely to develop a helpless orientation. They feel worthy when they are successful and unworthy when they fail.

People who hold an "incremental theory" of intelligence or who have a growth mind-set tend to believe that with effort and guidance everyone can increase and improve their intellectual abilities. Thus, they thrive on challenges and are even motivated to learn by them. As

Dweck (2000) noted, if you believe your intelligence can be increased, then "why waste time worrying about looking smart or dumb, when you could be becoming smarter?" (p. 3). Students with a growth mind-set feel smart when they fully engage with new tasks, seek to attain mastery, push and stretch their skills, and vigorously strive to solve problems. They actually prefer challenging tasks because those challenges give them the opportunity to raise their self-esteem by rising to the occasion and solving the problems before them. Growth mind-set students are more likely to attain their performance goals because they are more willing to persist and invest the time, energy, and effort it takes to perform well (Dweck, 2000).

The research of Dweck and her colleagues indicated that students with a fixed mind-set are at a disadvantage in challenging academic situations. They are less likely to fully embrace academic challenges or to be willing to struggle and persist to solve problems. Thus, students' beliefs about intelligence can actually influence their behavior. Students with a fixed mind-set are more likely to retreat in the face of difficult tasks. Also, the fixed mind-set may lead to self-handicapping behavior in which students risk failure (e.g., putting off writing a paper until the last minute) to save their view of their intelligence (Rhodewalt, 1994). They can blame their poor performance on lack of effort instead of lack of ability. In contrast, students with a growth mind-set are more likely to tolerate uncertainty, persist, and monitor and instruct themselves as they seek out answers and solutions over time. (For more reading about the mastery and helpless orientations and the fixed and growth mind-sets, see Dweck 2000, 2006.)

An important difference between doctoral students with a fixed versus a growth mind-set is that the former expect the ability to do a dissertation to show up before they have ever completed a dissertation. It is as if they are waiting for the ability to do a dissertation to show up, knock on their door, and give them permission to perform. In contrast, doctoral students with a growth mind-set understand that the ability to do a dissertation is something that they are earning day by day, struggle by struggle. They will cultivate the ability to do a dissertation through the experience of doing their own work over time.

It is important to stop and consider which view of intelligence you hold. Do you have a fixed or a growth mind-set when it comes to your own intellectual abilities? Do you maintain more of a fixed mind-set about some areas of academic work such as writing or statistics but a more growth-oriented mind-set about other areas, such as designing interventions or interviewing study participants? People do not necessarily have a strict fixed or growth mind-set across the broad spectrum of academic and intellectual abilities. It is possible that you have a fixed mind-set about some abilities and a growth mind-set about others. You may also notice that you may have a fixed or growth mind-set about other human qualities and capacities, such as artistic, musical, or athletic ability; personality; or relationships (see Dweck, 2006). The growth mind-set does not assume that anyone can achieve anything but rather that the true potential of a human being is unknown (Dweck, 2000). It is worth taking note of your beliefs about intellectual ability and how they may be holding you back from engaging fully in your dissertation and actually becoming smarter. Your dissertation can be an experience of great intellectual growth for you. But first you need to believe that last statement to be true. In chapter 3, I discuss strategies for cultivating a growth mind-set.

THINKING TRAP 3: COGNITIVE FUSION

So far you have learned about common thinking problems that can detract from your dissertation experience. Beyond being negative, these thoughts are problematic because they tend to be accepted at face value, as if the thoughts are what they say they are. The work of Hayes and his colleagues (e.g., Hayes, 2004; Hayes & Smith, 2005; Hayes, Strosahl, & Wilson, 1999) indicated that a significant way humans can be trapped by their thinking is through a process called *cognitive fusion*. Cognitive fusion is both important to understand and challenging to explain. So take your time to understand this concept.

There are two pervasive forms of cognitive fusion that are important for you to understand. The first is called *buying your thoughts,* which is essentially the process whereby you accept your thoughts (or interpretations of events) as if they were literal representations of an actual event and you respond to thoughts about an event as if they were the event themselves (Eifert & Forsyth, 2005; Hayes et al., 1999). For example, if you are struggling to develop a sound theoretical framework for your dissertation study, you will automatically make an evaluation of the situation. Your evaluation may include thoughts such as "I can't do this work. It is too hard" or "I am not smart enough." Cognitive fusion is the subtle and insidious process in which you fuse your thoughts or evaluations with the event you are experiencing (in this case, difficulty developing a theoretical framework). Thus, the evaluation and the event become fused. You "buy the thought" at face value, not recognizing that the struggle to develop a framework is an experience you are having and the self-doubting interpretation is an evaluation or thought about the event. As a consequence of buying this thought about the event, you are more likely to feel anxious and respond to the work you need to do as if your thoughts are the event. When the thought and the event are disentangled, you recognize that you are having self-doubting thoughts about developing a theoretical framework. The evaluation and the event are not one and the same. Your evaluation is a thought, nothing more, nothing less (Eifert & Forsyth, 2005).

The experience of fusion also occurs with emotions. For example, if you have the feeling of being sad or anxious, fusion occurs when you fuse the feeling you are experiencing with your evaluation of yourself. Such fusion sounds like "I am depressed" or "I am anxious." Instead of recognizing that you are having sad or anxious feelings (e.g., "I am having the feeling of depression or anxiety"), you attach yourself to a label or evaluation of your emotional state and then it is as if you are your evaluation. You and the label become one and the same in your mind (Hayes et al., 1999).

The second form of cognitive fusion is called the *yes-but* trap. This trap occurs when your thoughts and feelings become justifications for not taking action in your life. For example, students often tell me some version of the following, "I want to write more but I feel so overwhelmed." These students are actually saying that writing more cannot occur along with the feeling of being overwhelmed. By saying "but I feel so overwhelmed," the students are essentially making the first part of the sentence go away as if the commitment to writing is not there in the face of being overwhelmed. The students do not realize that they can write *and* feel overwhelmed at the same time. Other common examples of the yes-but trap I hear among students are

- "I need to make progress on my dissertation, but I have so much else going on now."
- "I am struggling to write my literature review, but I am scared to talk to my advisor."
- "I need to get motivated, but I just don't feel like working."
- "I need to finish entering my data, but the work is so tedious and boring."
- "I want to finish my dissertation, but I am scared about what comes next."

In these statements, the "but" part of the phrase becomes a justification for not acting and moving the dissertation forward. I encourage you to consider whether you fall into the yes-but or buying your thoughts traps of cognitive fusion. Cognitive fusion is ingrained in the language habits of human beings (Eifert & Forsyth, 2005), but you need not remain stuck in these traps. In chapter 3, you will learn cognitive defusion strategies to help you disentangle your evaluations from events and stop using "but" as a justification for inaction.

THINKING TRAP 4: NONACCEPTANCE AND CONTROL OF YOUR THINKING

As a result of reading this chapter so far, you are likely examining your own ways of thinking. You may be more aware of the content of your thoughts about doing a dissertation than you were before reading this chapter. I believe understanding how you think and how it can get you into trouble with your dissertation is important. Yet there can also be a pitfall to this focus on thinking. Sometimes when students learn more about cognitive errors, the fixed and growth mind-sets, and cognitive fusion they unknowingly begin to demand that they should not get caught in these thinking traps. It is important for you to know that I am teaching you about thinking traps because I want you to be aware of them, not because I believe you should not have them. All human beings experience thinking traps, and judging yourself for being human will not free you from these traps. It is true that thinking traps can interfere with your dissertation. It is also true that it can be desirable to change and be more accepting of thinking traps. Still, I caution you against evaluating them as bad, wrong, or unacceptable. In fact, demanding that you should not experience thinking traps is a trap in and of itself (Ellis, 2001). Such demands leave you feeling bad and often lead to efforts to control or suppress unpleasant and unwanted thoughts.

As Hayes and Smith (2005) discussed in more detail, the very effort to suppress thoughts makes them more central to your thinking. By trying not to think certain thoughts, you tell yourself "don't think X" and thereby create a verbal rule that includes the thought you do not want to think (X). So the rule itself will tend to evoke the unwanted thought. Also, when you check to see whether your efforts to control the negative thought are working, you will remember the unwanted thought. In this way, efforts to control or suppress thoughts can and often do increase the presence of the very thought you do not want to think (Hayes & Smith, 2005).

Humans are particularly vulnerable to trying to control their thinking because they are used to being able to control their external world. If your computer is not working properly, you can just get rid of your computer, buy a new one, or have it repaired. Through conscious, deliberate effort you can often rid yourself of unwanted external experiences. However, in our internal world such control efforts often fail. As Eifert and Forsyth (2005) pointed out, you cannot go inside your brain and control what you are thinking. In fact, trying to control your thoughts and rid yourself of those you do not want to have will likely ensure that you continue to experience those thoughts. In addition, nonacceptance of your thoughts and the consequent effort to control thinking can contribute to behavior that interferes with your dissertation progress. As is discussed more in chapter 3, holding a more accepting stance toward thinking traps will help you reduce the impact of these traps far more than a demanding, nonaccepting stance (Hayes et al., 1999).

Feeling Traps

Doctoral students are also vulnerable to feeling or emotional traps whereby negative emotions such as anxiety, depression, and anger diminish quality of life and interfere with their dissertation progress. Let's look at three emotional traps that I believe are important for you to understand.

FEELING TRAP 1: THE EMOTION–THINKING DISCONNECT

The first feeling trap is being unaware of the connection between emotions and thoughts. It is tempting to believe that your negative emotions are caused directly by the adverse or challenging situations you experience. For example, you may believe that feeling discouraged or depressed is caused by your lack of productivity or difficulty writing. Yet situations such as these do not cause negative emotions in and of themselves. Your thoughts or evaluations about the situations influence your emotional experience (Ellis, 2001).

Here are some examples of how students' thoughts about common academic challenges can influence emotions. In response to the need to do a quality dissertation and meet department requirements (and the desire most students have to be approved of and viewed as intelligent), you may make demands that you absolutely must be intelligent, productive, and motivated when it comes to your dissertation. Anxiety and depression are common consequences of being unable to meet your unrealistic demands, especially when you believe failing to meet your demands is awful or unbearable. When you procrastinate and do not live up to your demands about using time wisely or being productive, it is easy to feel guilty, anxious, or ashamed of your lack of productivity. If you keep telling yourself that your advisor is harsh and ineffective as a chairperson, then you may struggle to view your advisor in any other way and end up feeling angry and resentful. If you have overgeneralized and concluded that you are intellectually inadequate, you are likely to be worried in many academic situations and feel depressed or anxious any time you perform below your standards or the standards of others. You may also experience anxiety and feelings of depression as a consequence of overestimating negative outcomes (both in terms of frequency and severity) and underestimate your ability to effectively cope with such outcomes.

When you are unaware of the connection between your thinking and your emotions, you may become stuck believing it is the situation, not your interpretation of the situation that is causing your emotional pain. It is often easier to challenge, change, or be more accepting of your thoughts than it is to change adverse situations. When you experience negative emotions (you may not be certain how to label the emotion but you likely know when you feel bad), notice what thinking traps may be contributing to your emotional experience. By identifying the source of your negative emotions, you may be able to improve how you feel by changing your thinking. Of course, there are times when the source of your emotional pain is unclear or knowing the source does little to help diminish unwanted emotions. At these times, as discussed in chapter 3, it is worth adopting a more accepting attitude toward negative emotions, noticing their presence and continuing to move in a directed way toward your dissertation goals.

FEELING TRAP 2: NONACCEPTANCE OF FEELINGS

A second feeling trap is the lack of acceptance students often have of their negative emotions. According to Ellis (2001), human beings often demand that they should not have unpleasant or painful emotional experiences. I have certainly witnessed firsthand how students tell themselves that experiencing emotions such as depression, anxiety, anger, or shame is awful. As a result of their demands and intolerance, they struggle to accept, fully feel, and experience the negative emotions that they are in fact experiencing. It is important to realize that how you evaluate your emotions will directly impact how motivated you are to cope effectively with the event that precipitated your emotional distress (Ellis, 2001).

Having negative beliefs about negative emotions usually leads people to become further entrenched in feeling badly and behaving in ways that intensify the challenges they are experiencing in the first place (Mullin, 2000). For example, let's say you are asked to make significant revisions to your methodology chapter and then you feel ashamed about being asked to make the revisions. You might tell yourself that feeling ashamed is terrible and that you cannot handle feeling this emotion. Therefore, you avoid even attempting to make the revisions for fear that you will experience shame if you fail to effectively revise the chapter. Experiencing negative emotions on your dissertation journey is largely inevitable. The more accepting and willing you are for those emotions to exist, the less power they will have to interfere with your dissertation progress. I know it may seem that you need to control your negative emotions before you can be productive, but as you will see the effort to control negative emotions is what often interferes the most with productivity.

FEELING TRAP 3: EMOTIONAL CONTROL

As a consequence of nonacceptance of emotions, students are often led directly to the third feeling trap of emotional control. Just as efforts to suppress unwanted thoughts can lead to more unwanted thoughts, efforts to suppress unwanted feelings can result in more unwanted feelings (Hayes & Smith, 2005). When you try to control or suppress emotions such as anxiety or sadness, the focus on *not* having those emotional experiences includes a focus on the unwanted experience itself. By telling yourself "don't feel anxious," for example, before an upcoming meeting with your advisor, those feelings (and the thoughts associated with those feelings) become more salient (Eifert & Forsyth, 2005). You are so concerned with not being anxious that you become focused on monitoring yourself for any sign of anxiety. Thus, any indication that you are anxious is likely to intensify the very feelings you are trying to control.

Remember, we cannot control our internal experience of emotions the same way that we can control many external unwanted experiences. Unlike a poorly working computer that you can get rid of through conscious effort, you cannot deliberately go into your head and rid yourself of unwanted emotions. Your efforts to control your emotions are likely to amplify the unwanted ones (Hayes & Smith, 2005). Graduate students (and human beings in general) are quite vulnerable to the thinking and feeling traps of control. As you will see, these traps contribute significantly to behaving traps that can have a profound impact on your dissertation experience.

Behaving Traps

The thinking and emotion traps experienced by graduate students have significant consequences: They ensnare students in behaving traps that diminish productivity, interfere with learning, and make it harder for students to consistently work toward their goal of finishing their dissertation. Let's look at two common behaving traps.

BEHAVING TRAP 1: BEHAVIOR–THINKING–FEELING DISCONNECT

Just as students are often unaware of the connection between their thoughts and feelings, they are likely to be unaware of the connections between their behavior, thoughts, and feelings. The first behavior trap is not recognizing how your behavior, especially the behavior that interferes with your dissertation, is influenced by your thoughts and feelings. For example, a common behavioral issue among graduate students is procrastination. Unaware of the connections among your thoughts, feelings, and behavior, it may appear as if a character flaw such as laziness causes your procrastination. Yet, procrastination and laziness are not the same. Procrastination is the act of directing energy and effort toward alternate activities. Knaus (2002) pointed out that "laziness implies an unwillingness to use effort or energy, or an apathy for activity" (p. 21). I have never met a graduate student who was truly apathetic toward his or her dissertation. Sure, there might be fleeting days or moments where you feel apathetic. When you are procrastinating, though, you are actively directing your energy and effort away from dissertation activities toward other activities. The cause of procrastination is not laziness but rather the need to escape thoughts such as "It should not be so hard for me to write" or "I am worried what my advisor will think" and consequent emotions such as shame and anxiety.

Negative thoughts and feelings fuel procrastination. A typical pathway from thinking to procrastination is when graduate students create excessive demands for their academic performance, intellectual ability, and the quantity or quality of work completed in a given time period. These demands lead to anxiety and fear. Thus, procrastination seems like an effective short-term strategy to avoid the pressure of meeting excessive and anxiety-provoking demands. Yet procrastination often keeps students locked in a vicious cycle of negative thoughts, emotions, and behavior. Making demands about the quality and quantity of work you can complete in a given time frame can seem like a good way to catch up and compensate for time spent procrastinating. You may rationalize to yourself that if you can live up to your demands, you can make up for lost time. Yet the demands are unrealistic and unattainable. Thus, you continue to procrastinate to relieve yourself of the pressure of living up your excessive demands. Following the next bout of procrastination, you escalate your demands even more. The excessive demands keep you stuck in a continual cycle of procrastination and failed attempts to motivate yourself with unrealistic expectations. In this way, the very strategy you use to end procrastination and increase productivity becomes the source of your procrastination and lack of productivity. This cycle is a good illustration of how negative thinking, emotions, and self-defeating behavior can trigger and continually reinforce each other.

As you can see in the case of procrastination, self-defeating behavior does not just happen as a consequence of doing a dissertation. It occurs as a result of the thoughts and feelings you have about doing a dissertation. Being unaware of the connections among your behavior, thoughts, and feelings leaves you vulnerable to being trapped in self-defeating behavior because you do not know the real cause. When you are engaging in behavior that interferes with your dissertation, I encourage you to look deeper and seek out the thoughts and emotions operating in the background. Being more accepting of negative thoughts and feelings and shifting your perspective when you can makes it easier to engage in productive dissertation behavior.

BEHAVING TRAP 2: EXPERIENTIAL AVOIDANCE

The thinking and feeling traps discussed in this chapter all contribute to the second behavioral trap: *experiential avoidance*. Experiential avoidance is any behavior that helps you avoid or escape any unwanted private experiences, such as thoughts, feelings, bodily sensations, memories, and behavioral predispositions (Hayes et al., 1999). (For the sake of brevity in this text, I will use the terms *thoughts* and *feelings*, but I want the reader to know that unwanted experiences may also be bodily sensations, memories, and behavioral predispositions.) Any behavior, such as overcommitting to research and teaching activities, avoiding your advisor, oversleeping, using drugs and alcohol, or making household chores or social events a priority, can be a means of experiential avoidance if the aim of the behavior is to avoid and escape unwanted private experiences associated with your dissertation. To help you better understand experiential avoidance, let's examine the two most common avoidance strategies I see among graduate students: procrastination and perfectionism.

Procrastination

As discussed earlier, *procrastination* is an active process of avoidance. Doctoral students are remarkably ingenious when it comes to finding ways to engage in the behavior of procrastination. There are the obvious procrastination strategies: checking e-mail, surfing the Internet, watching television, eating, sleeping, talking on the phone, reading books for pleasure, playing computer games, and socializing with friends. (There is nothing wrong with engaging in any of these activities. These activities only become an issue when you consistently engage in them as away to avoid your dissertation.) There are also the procrastination activities that at face value seem like dissertation activities, such as getting your work environment "just right," conducting endless literature reviews on the Internet, organizing research materials, or reading more sources when you really need to be writing. What makes these activities acts of procrastination is that they are peripheral activities to the real work you know you need to do. To the outside world, it looks like you are working on your dissertation, and for a short time you can rationalize and convince yourself that you are indeed making progress. But in reality, you are actually procrastinating. The real work you need to do is usually the more challenging work of new writing, thinking through ideas, and problem solving, which may trigger negative thoughts and emotions. And because students tend to believe that they should not be having such thoughts and emotions, they engage in behavior that helps them avoid or escape what they do not want to think or feel.

Sometimes it is useful to create some distance from your dissertation and a particular challenge you are facing. Answers and solutions may come more easily to you when you have had some time away from your dissertation. Many students tell me that they have great ideas in the shower, drifting off to sleep at night, or at random when they are disengaged from their dissertation work. Yet there is a difference between giving yourself a needed break from intellectual engagement and procrastinating because the work seems too hard, boring, or unpleasant. If you are honest with yourself, you will know the difference.

Perfectionism

Perfectionism is another form of experiential avoidance. Perfectionism is maintaining unrealistically high standards that are impossible to attain (Hewitt & Flett, 1991). Perfectionism among doctoral students usually involves making absolute demands about their intellectual capacity and academic performance. For example, many students demand that they must write perfectly or have their work be above criticism. Overall, perfectionist students tell themselves that it would be unacceptable to be viewed by others as flawed or inadequate—especially intellectually inadequate. They go beyond having a healthy desire to be successful and rigidly demand perfect performance. Such demands are unrealistic and contribute to self-doubting thoughts, negative emotions, and perfectionist behavior (Ellis, 2001).

Perfectionist behavior is performed in an effort to avoid feared thoughts and feelings. For example, if you fear being criticized by your committee, you may obsess about writing perfectly crafted sentences or delay turning in your work in an effort to perfect it before anyone else can read it. If you fear being questioned about your statistical analysis strategy, then you may rerun your analysis over and over to try to get it "just right." In being a perfectionist you are not avoiding the event of being criticized or questioned about your work. Rather, you are avoiding the thoughts (e.g., you are not smart enough, you should always excel) and feelings (e.g., anxiety, fear) associated with the feedback.

The Problem With Avoidance

Procrastination and perfectionism, like any avoidance behavior, are problematic because they keep you from being meaningfully engaged in your dissertation. These avoidance strategies do seem to work in the short run in that they offer temporary relief from unwanted thoughts and feelings. If you avoid or aim to perfect your dissertation, it seems as if you can avoid discomfort and pain. Yet such avoidance quickly becomes a behavioral trap, not the solution you are seeking. Your effort to suppress, control, and avoid negative thoughts and feelings interferes with being able to engage with your dissertation, and that is a problem in and of itself. Not only do you experience the pain of unwanted thoughts and feelings, you also experience the pain of not being able to move your dissertation forward. The less progress you make, the more likely you are to experience negative thoughts and feelings. If you continue to be unwilling to experience those thoughts and feelings, you will likely continue to engage in experiential avoidance.

Avoidance is particularly unfortunate because when you move away from dissertation work that challenges you (and its associated thoughts and feelings), you may reinforce the fixed mind-set and negative beliefs about your capacity to earn a PhD. You are not able to struggle with the material, think, explore ideas and concepts, talk things over with others, revise your work, and ultimately rise to the occasion to find an answer, solution, or way to overcome the obstacle or intellectual challenge you are facing. Every time you choose to check your e-mail, aim to perform perfectly, or engage in other avoidance behavior, you may be cutting yourself off from accessing your true intellectual potential.

Sometimes you may need to wade through a period of confusion or struggle while you try to figure out answers, solutions, or an appropriate course of action. It can be challenging to hang in there and stay present, but when you do you are likely to be rewarded with the discovery that you are smarter, more capable, and more creative than you know. You can come to see that intelligence is in fact malleable and that persistence gives you the reward of greater skill, experience, and competency (Dweck, 2006). It is true that sometimes the struggle may last days or even weeks. You may need to ask other people for their input and ideas and continue to think, read, and write until the answers become apparent. It is not necessarily a fun or pretty process, but this struggle is the way the true intellectual and creative process works, whether you like it or believe it should be that way.

Graduate students often use the presence of unwanted thoughts and feelings as a justification for inaction. Indeed, in our culture it is generally accepted that you need to have positive thoughts and feelings to be able to engage fully in life (Eifert & Forsyth, 2005). I often witness graduate students who are stuck believing that they need to change or stop their thoughts or emotions before they can work. Certainly, there are times when you can develop a new outlook or perspective on yourself and being a graduate student. Yet such change often comes slowly or is difficult to attain, making it important to become more accepting of your own private dissertation experience. If you become more willing to experience negative thoughts and feelings, then you can reach a place in life where they can be present at the same time you are working on your dissertation. I am actually saying that you can have negative thoughts and feelings and work on your dissertation. You can be anxious and work. You can doubt your abilities and work. The more accepting and willing you are to have negative thoughts and feelings as you work on your dissertation, the easier it will be for you to stay engaged in the work and avoid the trap of experiential avoidance.

Freeing Yourself

Graduate school is a context where thinking, feeling, and behaving traps are virtually impossible to avoid. These unwanted private experiences are a part of being human (Hayes & Smith, 2005). No matter how you have struggled up until this point, you can learn to develop a more accepting and flexible outlook on your dissertation experience and free yourself from these traps. Chapter 3 offers cognitive, emotional, and behavioral strategies that will help you be more productive, learn more, and even enjoy the dissertation journey.

Freeing Yourself From Thinking, Feeling, and Behaving Traps

3

E ven though it is likely that you have experienced some or all of the thinking, feeling, and behaving traps discussed in chapter 2, freedom from these traps is possible. No matter how stuck you may be or how unpleasant or challenging the dissertation process has been for you, there is great reason for hope and optimism. I have witnessed hundreds of doctoral students find their way out of all sorts of traps. It sometimes took great courage, but even students who came to me overwhelmed and demoralized found a way to move forward and cross the PhD finish line. Freeing yourself is not necessarily easy. Yet your efforts can lead to a meaningful change in your life. You can develop a more accepting, flexible, and compassionate view of yourself and the dissertation process. You can become more willing to experience the negative thoughts and emotions while at the same time taking action to move your dissertation forward. My hope is that the strategies offered here will help you on your dissertation journey and life beyond graduate school.

This chapter is organized into six sections, each offering you a different strategy to address thinking, feeling, and behaving traps. In general, each of the strategies can be used to impact any trap directly or indirectly. The strategies in this chapter will lay the groundwork for the more concrete behavioral strategies described in chapters 4 through 8 that will help you finish your dissertation once and for all. Some of the strategies I recommend are relatively simple, and you can begin using them today. Others require more effort and a sustained commitment. I encourage you to give these strategies a real chance to take hold over time so they can have the greatest possible impact.

Strategy 1: Develop an Accepting Stance Toward Thinking, Feeling, and Behaving Traps

An important strategy to free yourself from thinking, feeling, and behaving traps is to first and foremost develop an accepting stance toward the occurrence of these traps. As discussed in chapter 2, you can expect to experience negative thoughts and feelings and self-defeating behavior at some point or even at many points on the dissertation journey. Even though the experience of these traps is quite normal and difficult to avoid, you may believe that you should not be experiencing thoughts, feelings, or behavior that interfere with your dissertation. For example, you may believe you should not doubt yourself, feel afraid, or procrastinate. Yet the presence of these thoughts, feelings, and behaviors would be less problematic if you were more accepting when they do show up in your life.

My use of acceptance comes primarily from a form of psychotherapy called Acceptance and Commitment Therapy (ACT, pronounced like the word "act" not A-C-T). ACT is a behavior therapy approach developed by Steven Hayes and his colleagues (see Hayes, Strosahl, & Wilson, 1999). The aim of ACT is to help people "accept themselves and others with compassion, choose valued directions for their lives and commit to action that leads them in those directions" (Eifert & Forsyth, 2005, pp. 6–7). Acceptance in the context of ACT does not mean toleration or resignation to thinking, feeling, or behaving traps or to pain or difficult life circumstances (Hayes & Smith, 2005). It is not passive acceptance in which you give up taking action in important areas of your life that you can control. Acceptance does not mean you condone your experience; nor does it mean that you give up or fail to take responsibility. Rather, acceptance is about being willing to fully and courageously experience everything, including the unwanted private experiences of negative thoughts and feelings (Eifert & Forsyth, 2005). It is a stance you take toward your dissertation experience that is about behavior and action.

Acceptance is where you stop demanding that you should not have pain or unwanted experiences and are willing to allow them to be present as you work on your dissertation. Such willingness is in the service of being in the moment with unwanted experiences instead of reacting to them through behavior that is designed to avoid or escape the unwanted experiences (Hayes & Smith, 2005). When you are unwilling to accept or come into contact with unwanted thoughts and feelings then your only choice is to avoid or react to those thoughts and feelings. Thus, the full repertoire of behavior in which you are willing to engage becomes limited. Experiential avoidance such as procrastination or perfectionism can seem like a good way to escape pain and unwanted thoughts and feelings. Yet such avoidance actually creates suffering. Not only do you have the pain of the unwanted thoughts and feelings but you now also have the pain caused by avoiding your dissertation and not moving toward an important values-driven goal.

Active acceptance empowers you to finish your dissertation and gives you the remarkable freedom to fully experience whatever thoughts and feelings arise along the way (Eifert & Forsyth, 2005). For example, a typical response to the thought "I don't know how to organize my ideas" is to avoid writing. When you can observe the thought and can see it as a thought, then you have more choice about how you want to behave. You can consider that the thought is merely an evaluation of yourself and your situation and recognize that you still have the freedom to write even in the presence of that thought. If you can be more accepting and willing for anxiety to be present when you are working on your dissertation, then you are able to free up your energy from struggling against anxiety. Instead, you can use that energy to work on your dissertation even when anxiety is present. You do not have to live in fear of anxiety because you are willing to fully experience it when it occurs. Paradoxically, when you are more accepting of your thoughts and feelings, it more likely that you can change them for the better or experience them with less intensity (Ellis, 2001; Hayes et al., 1999). Yet the aim of acceptance is not to change your thoughts and feelings. It is to "acknowledge them without taking them as facts, approving or disapproving of them, or doing anything about them" (Eifert & Forsyth, 2005, p. 72) and take action toward your value-driven goals.

As Hayes and Smith (2005) pointed out, clearly we are not talking about accepting situations, events, or behaviors that are readily changeable or clearly destructive. If you are abusing drugs or alcohol or harming yourself or others in some way, these situations do not call for acceptance. Something does need to be changed. Yet actively accepting the pain, thoughts, and emotions driving you to engage in the destructive behavior is called for. In fact, such acceptance may help you change the negative behavior you are using to cope with pain and unwanted thoughts and emotions. Likewise, if you have been procrastinating, being more accepting of the thoughts and feelings that contribute to avoidance may help you be more productive. On the other hand, if your advisor is excessively abusive and critical, accepting his or her behavior is not called for. You can be accepting of how you think and feel in response to your advisor's behavior, but there is no good reason to allow someone to mistreat and abuse you.

As I wrote this book, I had many opportunities to practice acceptance. When negative thoughts appeared in my head, I imagined that I was welcoming them into the room with me. I thought of it the following way: Being unwilling to experience certain thoughts and feelings is like leaning up against my office door trying to keep them out. I have to use my energy to keep my negative thoughts and emotions at bay. Meanwhile, my computer, notes, and materials for writing this book are over at my desk without me. I can't sit at the desk and write my book because I am leaning up against the door trying to keep undesired thoughts and feelings out.

When I open the door, it as if I am saying, "Welcome, unwanted thoughts and feelings, have a seat. I was expecting you, because I have noticed that you frequently show up when I aim to write. Well, you can hang out as long as you like, but I'll be over at my desk writing." By welcoming and accepting my thoughts and feelings as thoughts and feelings, I refuse to fuse myself with these experiences. They do not define me or require me to control them. I am willing to witness that I have thoughts and feelings I do not like *and* choose to move forward, taking one step at a time toward completing this book.

Developing an accepting stance can be challenging and even feel frightening. Students often believe that if they are accepting, they will become completely unmotivated. They believe being nonaccepting of their experience (demanding that they do not have the experience they are having) is an important way to motivate themselves. It can seem as if trying to control and suppress unwanted thoughts, feelings, and behavior is an effective way to win the war against these experiences (and return to your dissertation work). But how well does waging this nonaccepting war really work? Does it actually lead to motivation and productivity? Remember that by acceptance, I do not mean passive resignation or condoning procrastination or other self-defeating behavior. I mean being willing to accept the thoughts and feelings driving unproductive behavior and then courageously taking action that is consistent with your values, commitments, and goals. In this way, you step off the battlefield and stop fighting with your unwanted private experiences. You can use your energy to actually work on your dissertation.

An important way to develop a more accepting stance is to be mindful of unwanted thoughts and feelings that can lead to behavior traps. Mindfulness involves observing and attending to your current experience (i.e., thoughts, feelings, and sensations you are experiencing in the moment). Mindfulness also involves holding a curious, open, and accepting stance toward what is being experienced (Eifert & Forsyth, 2005). Mindful acceptance creates space for you to think, feel, and witness the thoughts and emotions that interfere with your dissertation progress.

You are aware of the presence of your thoughts and feelings as mere thoughts and feelings and willing for them to be present whether or not you like them or think they should exist. Thus, you have greater freedom to choose how you want to behave instead of responding to your thoughts and feeling through automatic and habitual avoidant or self-defeating behavior (Eifert & Forsyth, 2005).

Acceptance and mindfulness are ways of engaging with life. Each is a practice you cultivate, not an outcome or a destination. Meditation is probably one of the most common ways people engage in this practice, but it is not the only way. An extensive review of the philosophy of acceptance and mindfulness and how to practice them is beyond the scope of this text; however, I do offer a practice exercise that many of my clients find useful (see Exercise 3.1). For readers who are interested in further exploring the ideas of acceptance and mindfulness, I highly recommend reading *Get Out of Your Mind and Into Your Life* (2005) by Steven Hayes and Spencer Smith and listening to Tara Brach's (2000) audio program *Radical Self-Acceptance*.

EXERCISE 3.1

Practice Mindfulness

Read the following script several times until you feel comfortable following the instructions. You may want someone else to read it to you or to record the instructions and play it back for your practice. Do not worry about getting distracted during the practice. Getting distracted is normal. All there is to do is bring your attention back to the exercise.

- Get into a comfortable position sitting or lying down. This is a chance to rest but not to sleep. Take your time and move slowly. Allow yourself to fully observe and witness your own experience. Allow your eyes to close gently.
- Take several deep breaths, letting them become slightly deeper with each breath. Feel the air coming in through your nose, filling your chest and belly. Then take your time, slowly release each breath.
- Bring your attention to your chest and belly. Place one hand on your chest and the other on your belly. Can you feel yourself breathing? What is it like? Are you breathing fast or slow? Spend some time attending to your breathing. Keep bringing your attention back to your breath, noticing your chest and belly rising and falling. Breathe in through your nose and out through your mouth. Notice what it feels like. Reverse the pattern and breathe in through your mouth and out through your nose. Notice what it feels like.
- As you breathe in and out, become aware of your body. Notice how your body feels and where it makes contact with your chair or bed. Take your time and feel your feet and legs. Breathe deeply and bring your attention to any sensations in your feet and legs. How are they positioned? What do you notice? How do your feet and legs feel against the bed or on the floor and chair?
- Move your attention to your torso. Feel your back against the chair or bed. What does it feel like? Observe any sensations? Bring your awareness to the feelings up your back, around your sides, and up the front of your torso. As you breathe, take note of any sensations you experience. Take your time.

(continued)

EXERCISE 3.1 (*Continued*)

▪ Bring your attention to your arms and shoulders. How are your arms and shoulders positioned on the chair or bed? Let them be as they are. As you breathe notice any sensations as you move your attention slowly from your fingertips to your shoulders. Observe your fingers, hands, lower arms, upper arms, and shoulders.

▪ Move your attention to your face. Bring awareness to your brow. Is it smoothed and relaxed or crinkled up and tense? Let it be as it is and just notice it how it is. Now bring your attention to your nose. Breathing in and out through your nose, how does it feel? Pay attention to how the air feels coming in and out. What do you notice? Bring your attention to your jaw. Is it tense or relaxed? No need to change it. Just observe it, notice how it feels. Moving to your mouth, notice how it is positioned. Is it open? Closed? Pursed? Is the inside of your mouth wet or dry?

▪ Now bring your attention to your head and neck. How is your head positioned? Notice if it is aligned with your spine. There is no need to adjust it. Observe and notice any sensations in your head and neck.

▪ Now bring your attention to your mind. Consider your dissertation for a moment. Imagine what you are working on now. What thoughts come to mind? Take your time and observe what thoughts appear. If your mind seems blank, that is okay. There is no need to force anything. Rehearse whatever thoughts come up using the statements, "My mind is telling me . . ." and "I am having the thought that. . . ." Spend as much time observing thoughts as you like. Breathe into your chest and belly, and, with each breath, imagine you are creating space for your thoughts. Witness each thought as a thought. In your mind, let yourself, even for a just a moment, stand apart from your thoughts and let your experience be your experience. Take your time, breathing, creating space, and letting thoughts be thoughts.

▪ Now bring your attention to your body again. Consider your dissertation for a moment. Imagine what you are working on now. What feelings do you experience? If nothing comes up, there is no need to force anything. Just observe what is there naturally. Take your time and notice what feelings you experience. Observe whatever feelings come up using the statements, "I am having the feeling of . . ." and "I am having the experience of. . . ." Spend as much time observing feelings as you like. Breathe into your chest and belly and with each breath, imagine you are creating space for your feelings. Witness each feeling as a feeling. In your mind, let yourself, even for a just a moment, stand apart from the feelings you experience, and let your experience be your experience. Take your time, breathing, creating space, and letting feelings be feelings.

▪ Now bring your attention to your body again. Consider your dissertation for a moment. Imagine what you are working on now. What bodily sensations do you experience? Anything in your head, stomach, chest, back? If nothing comes up, there is no need to force anything. Just observe what is there naturally. Take your time and notice what body sensations you experience. Take note of any sensations that come up using the statements, "I am having the sensation of . . ." and "I am having the experience of. . . ." Spend as much time observing bodily sensations as you like. Breathe into your chest and belly and with each breath, imagine you are creating space for any bodily sensations you are experiencing. Witness each sensation as a sensation. In your mind, let yourself, even for a just a moment, stand apart from the sensations you experience, and let your experience be your experience. Take your time, breathing, creating space, and letting sensations be sensations.

▪ When you are ready, gradually bring your attention back to the sounds around you. Take a moment to create an intention to bring this sense of allowing and acceptance of your experience into the present moment. Slowly open your eyes, gradually raising your gaze from the floor to being fully back in the room.

Exercise 3.1, on mindfulness, is adapted from the work of Eifert and Forsyth (2005), Hanh (2003), and Hayes and Smith (2005). As you practice this exercise, I encourage you to let go of evaluating your "progress" or making judgments about whether or not it is working. This exercise is a chance to practice again and again being in the moment with the thoughts, feelings, bodily sensations, memories, and behavioral drives that you experience in connection to your dissertation and your life.

Before you begin practicing this exercise I want to point out that your mind cannot understand the experience of acceptance but you as a human being can (Hayes & Smith, 2005). Acceptance is an experiential not a cognitive phenomenon. Here is an analogy to help you understand what I mean. Recall the experience of learning to ride a bicycle. When you learn to ride a bicycle, you are given instructions and tips on achieving balance and successfully riding. Your mind understanding the instructions does not translate into having the experience of balance and being able to ride a bicycle. You have to keep trying to ride the bicycle (and usually fall a bunch of times) until that magic moment occurs where everything comes together and you have the experience of balance. Acceptance is a similar phenomenon. The best way to develop the capacity to be accepting is to practice it and let the experience evolve over time.

As you practice Exercise 3.1, be gentle, compassionate, and nonjudgmental. You cannot pass or fail this exercise (or any exercise in this book actually) you can only experience it. Practice even if you believe "These kinds of exercises do not work for me," "I don't have time to practice mindfulness," or "My mind is too busy or anxious for this to make a difference." Buying those thoughts will only keep you stuck in a nonaccepting state. Your mind will generate lots of thoughts during this practice. That is what minds do. Simply note that thoughts are flowing through your mind, and practice bringing yourself back to the present moment by observing your thoughts. You may have to bring your attention back over and over and over again and that it is okay as mindfulness is a practice not an outcome.

Strategy 2: Cognitive Defusion

An important thinking trap discussed in chapter 2 is cognitive fusion with a focus on two pervasive forms of fusion: *buying your thoughts* and the *yes-but trap*. Buying your thoughts is when you fuse an event (e.g., difficulty understanding a journal article) with your evaluation of the event (e.g., something must be wrong with me intellectually). Thus, the event and the thought (evaluative thought) about the event become one and the same and you buy the thought at face value. The yes-but trap happens when you justify your own inaction with your thoughts and feelings. An example of this trap is saying, "I'd like to run my data analysis this week but I don't know how." In this situation, the "but" part of the sentence becomes a justification for not working and may prevent the student from asking for help or pushing forward to figure it out him- or herself.

You can free yourself from the trap of cognitive fusion through a process called *cognitive defusion*. The purpose of defusion is to disentangle your evaluations or interpretations of events from your actual experience. Cognitive defusion will help you recognize and experience your evaluative thoughts and unwanted feelings as something that you have but that do not define you or your experience. Defusion is actually a way to practice mindfulness and acceptance as it helps you experience your thoughts and feelings as what they are (Eifert & Forsyth, 2005). Defusion can help you reach a place where you do not need to comply or resist your thoughts and feelings.

To free yourself from the trap of buying your thoughts, Hayes and Smith (2005) offered a simple technique whereby you practice your evaluative thoughts with the following phrase, "I am having the thought that. . . ." For example, consider the difference between the thoughts "my advisor does not support my work" (fused thought) and "I am having the thought that my advisor does not support my work" (defused thought). In the defused statement, you can create some distance and see it as merely a thought. You are able to look at your thoughts as an observer instead of only being able to look out at your world through the lens of your thought. Note that this technique can be used to address emotions and bodily sensations and it can be practiced with a variety of phrases shown in Exhibit 3.1.

This strategy may seem strange initially. But by practicing defusion, you can become better at experiencing evaluative thoughts and feelings as merely thoughts and feelings. You create distance between yourself and your experience so you can stop buying your thoughts and feelings at face value (Eifert & Forsyth, 2005). Consequently, you are more likely

EXHIBIT 3.1

Examples of Cognitive Defusion to Free Yourself From Buying Your Thoughts and Feelings

"**I am having the thought that** I should always be working on my dissertation."
"**My mind is telling me that** I don't have enough time to make any progress today."
"**I am buying the thought that** I need to feel highly inspired to work on my dissertation."
"**There goes my mind again thinking** my work needs to be perfect."
"**I am noticing that** my chest is tight, my stomach hurts, and I am feeling fearful."
"**My fears about** finding a job and what comes after my PhD **are knocking on the door.**"
"**I am having the feeling of** being depressed and overwhelmed."
"**I am having the experience of** shame about the time I spend procrastinating."

to experience greater freedom from your thinking and be able to engage in your dissertation in a more proactive way.

To free yourself from the yes-but trap, you can begin to use the word *and* instead of *but.* For example, notice the difference between the following thoughts: "I want to finish my statistical analysis *but* I have a busy week" and "I want to finish my statistical analysis *and* I have a busy week." In the first statement, the word *but* lets you off the hook. By telling yourself that doing your statistical analysis can not occur along with a busy week, you justify not working on your dissertation. By using *and* instead of *but* you can consider that you can have a busy week and work anyway.

Consider the statement, "I want to work on my dissertation and I feel scared." The statement encourages you to allow fear to be present when you work. It gives you the idea that you can conceivably work *and* be fearful. Fear no longer needs to be your justification for inaction. You do not have to wait for fear to subside or make it subside before your dissertation work can begin. That being said, I recognize there are times when your emotional experience is quite intense. You may need time and the support of others to be able to work while also having emotions that you experience as painful or difficult. I encourage you to bring an attitude of perseverance to cognitive defusion (as well as the other strategies in this chapter). Cognitive defusion takes practice, and over time it will help you develop a more accepting stance toward your own private experience of doing a dissertation and free you to work more proactively and productively.

Strategy 3: Cultivate a Growth Mind-Set

A key thinking trap discussed in chapter 2 is the belief that your intelligence is fixed and unchangeable. Some students have a *fixed* mind-set and believe intelligence is a largely unchangeable trait that dwells within them. Other students hold a *growth* mind-set and believe intelligence is malleable and that they can become smarter through their own efforts, hard work, and persistence (Dweck, 2006). According to Dweck (2006), the fixed mind-set creates an internal dialogue whereby students constantly judge their performance in terms of what it means about how smart they are. Success or positive feedback means they are smart. Failures, setbacks, or critical feedback means they are intellectually inadequate. Students with a growth mind-set also have an internal dialogue, observing and evaluating performance. But this dialogue is not about judging themselves. They are more focused on the implications of their performance for learning, growth, and taking constructive action. They want to know what they can learn from success, mistakes, and failures and how they can improve and develop themselves academically and intellectually. As a result, students with a growth mind-set are more motivated to learn, achieve more academically, and are ultimately more satisfied with the experience of being a student (Dweck 2000, 2006).

You may notice that you clearly have a fixed or a growth mind-set about intelligence. Alternatively, your mind-set may fluctuate depending on the kind of academic and intellectual tasks you are dealing with. If you have a fixed mind-set some or all of the time, you are not stuck with your beliefs about intelligence. There are a number of ways you can actively cultivate a growth mind-set.

The first step is to be aware of the existence of the two mind-sets and notice when you are operating in a fixed mind-set. Then you can seek to reorient yourself to the goal of learning. Notice when you fear that you are not smart enough, feel driven to prove your intelligence, or believe you should not have to exert a lot of effort when performing academic tasks. If you have a fixed mind-set or at least lean in that direction, you are not alone and there is no need to judge yourself. Many doctoral students were praised for their performance growing up and never learned about the value of effort and persistence or the importance of learning from mistakes. In addition, academic environments often inadvertently promote the idea that intelligence is fixed and contribute to students seeing their intelligence in a black-and-white manner (Dweck, 2006).

Rather than judging yourself when the fixed mind-set is present, I hope you will see an opportunity to cultivate a growth mind-set. When you face a dissertation challenge, you can ask yourself, "What can I learn?" "Who can I ask for help?" and "What other strategies and approaches can I try?" Remember that you once loved to learn. As a young child, you relentlessly pursued knowledge and new skills. You likely asked you parents "why?" thousands of times, wanting to understand the world better. The first time you tried to walk and fell down, you did not give up and assume walking was beyond your ability. You persisted and refined your ability to walk over time. Being a graduate student is a time when you are apt to "fall down" many times on your way to earning a doctoral degree. Let graduate school be a time when you can learn from each fall and aim to make learning an important priority over proving yourself and looking smart.

A second way you can cultivate a growth mind-set is to lower your work performance standards in a given work session. The fixed mind-set is fertile ground for making excessive demands of your performance. If you believe intelligence is unchangeable, you may demand that you absolutely must perform well each time you sit down to work on your dissertation. The pressure of needing to meet such high standards acts like a vice grip choking off your ability to think, explore ideas, write rough drafts, look at your work from different angles, ask for help, and do the deeper work of stretching your abilities. If you can lower your standards for your performance especially in the initial stages of your work, you give yourself the chance to be thoughtful and develop your work and learn over time. You can then apply higher standards to your work as time goes on. Students often believe that it will take longer to work with lower standards. But usually they have not stopped to consider how well the strategy of focusing on perfection and performance is really working for them. In reality, they often work at a slower pace, fearing rather than embracing struggle as a way to learn and develop themselves as researchers. By working with lower standards today, you can open yourself to the possibility that a focus on learning instead of performing is what actually improves performance and intelligence.

A third way to cultivate a growth mind-set is to focus on the learnable components of working on a dissertation. All the components of doing research such as writing, reading sources and discerning the relevance of theory and empirical findings to your work, devising a study method, data analysis, and interpreting your findings are learnable components of research. Often doctoral students assume that they *should* reach the dissertation stage already knowing how to complete such a project. Also, they tend to compare themselves with others who seem very talented at research and assume that because they do not have such talent, they never will. They seem to forget that faculty and other students all had to learn how to conduct research. Sure, research skills may come more easily and naturally to some people. But as Dweck (2006) so aptly pointed out, "just because some people can do something well with little or no training, it doesn't mean others can't do it (and sometimes do it better) with training" (p.70).

I encourage you to focus your attention on identifying and learning the learnable components of doing research and a dissertation. There is generally a protocol of rules, standards, and methods for conducting research. You are capable of learning that protocol even if you find it challenging. Struggle does not mean you cannot learn. On the contrary, it indicates that you are on the path to learning. Trust that with persistence and support from others, you can develop the research skills you need to complete your dissertation over time. Ask for help, persist, strategize, and put in the effort required to develop the ability to do a dissertation.

Letting go of the fixed mind-set can be challenging. For people with a fixed mind-set, proving yourself and focusing on performance is a well-practiced means to self-worth. It can be unsettling to reorient yourself toward embracing intellectual criticism and challenges instead of fearing them (Dweck, 2006). You may notice that your initial reaction to a dissertation obstacle or critical feedback is to feel inadequate or unworthy. But just because the fixed mind-set is present does not mean you cannot move toward a growth mind-set and take action aligned with the values (see Strategy 5) of persistence, growth, learning, and potential inherent in the growth mind-set.

Students often ask me how they can develop or maintain a growth mind-set when so many people around them (peers, advisors, and committee members, in particular) seem to operate with a fixed mind-set. This reality presents an important opportunity. You can clarify your own standard and definition of what makes you an intelligent, competent, and worthy human being instead of rating yourself based solely on external validation. When you can maintain a growth mind-set, academic disappointments have less power to render you inadequate in your own mind. A growth mind-set can actually help you be more resilient in an academic environment that may emphasize performance over learning. It is true that you do need to perform well and meet the expectations of your committee to successfully earn your degree. Yet when you emphasize learning, you can avoid the pitfall of having your dissertation experience be about proving yourself. If you cultivate a growth mind-set and make learning a priority, you will likely have a richer, more positive experience as a doctoral student and likely learn more.

Strategy 4: Creating Rational Coping Statements

In his writings, Albert Ellis encouraged people to develop rational coping statements as a way to reinforce a more positive, rational reality that is distinct from their negative beliefs. According to Ellis and MacLaren (1998), rational coping statements are affirmative, encouraging statements that reflect a more positive, accepting, honest, and rational outlook on yourself and your experience. Although the focus of this strategy is to help people change the content of their thinking, I use rational coping statements in a different way with my clients. I primarily emphasize their use as a way to affirm and support an accepting stance toward one's life and to promote cognitive defusion.

I also encourage students to embrace a growth mind-set as they create these statements when it is relevant. Here is an example of how a client named Joseph[1] used a rational coping statement to help himself. Joseph, who was seeking to earn a PhD in English, struggled a great deal with perfectionism. Although he would attempt to write on a daily basis, he spent most of the day procrastinating and becoming increasingly anxious. Joseph shared that when he was growing up his parents only expressed approval of him when he received perfect scores on exams and writing assignments. Consequently, Joseph internalized his

---

[1]All names and identifying information of students have been changed throughout this book. All client-specific material in this book is based on client experiences but is not an exact representation of any one specific client.

parents' excessive standards and demanded perfection from himself. His perfectionism was clearly interfering with his progress, and, at the rate he was writing, we determined it would take him many years to write his dissertation. On the basis of several conversations we had about his situation, Joseph created the following rational coping statement:

> If I am honest with myself, the way that I have been writing is very painful and slow and I am not getting much accomplished. My focus on perfection causes me to lose sight of the bigger picture and why I am seeking a PhD. I need to start writing and reminding myself that writing a rough sentence does not mean that others will rush to judge me or reject me, that I am not smart, or that I don't have what it takes to finish or pass my dissertation defense. Rough sentences are THE WAY to get ideas down on paper so that I can have something of substance to revise and refine so that I eventually have an entire dissertation written. Yes, it is true that I will likely feel uncomfortable and anxious as I approach writing in a new way. But I can be uncomfortable or anxious and let myself write rough drafts. If I don't give myself permission to write rough drafts, I will continue to spin my wheels and actually increase the likelihood that I will fail to finish graduate school. I am better off lowering my standards and giving myself the gift of just letting myself write. I can always raise my standards over time as I revise and improve my writing (provided I've written something in the first place so I can do the revisions).

Joseph read this statement out loud to himself on a daily basis, especially when he felt himself falling prey to perfectionistic thinking. I recommend that you review your rational coping statements as a way to help new you maintain a more flexible stance toward yourself and your dissertation.

Some additional examples of rational coping statements that you can use as models for creating your own follow in Exhibit 3.2.

EXHIBIT 3.2

Examples of Rational Coping Statements

Negative Belief: I am not smart enough. I should be smarter.
Rational Coping Statement: This belief has been in my life for a long time, and I have been viewing it as truth merely because the thought is present in my mind. Because I am only now starting to look at myself and my intelligence in a new light, I can expect that this thought will occur in my mind again and again. I can accept the presence of this thought without letting it persuade me to avoid my work. Also, if I think about intelligence as malleable then it is easier for me to hang in there when my dissertation work gets tough. I know that everyone struggles with his or her dissertation research at some time. By persisting in the face of struggle, I can explore new avenues, make discoveries, and eventually find solutions. I can tolerate feeling challenged and even enjoy the intellectual adventure of my dissertation. After all, I came to graduate school to learn and develop new skills and competencies.

(continued)

EXHIBIT 3.2 (*Continued*)

Negative Belief: I must be successful at everything I do or I risk being a worthless failure.
Rational Coping Statement: I would prefer to let go of this belief altogether as it has created a lot of pain in my life. But I recognize that it is likely I will continue to have this belief while I am in graduate school (and perhaps beyond). Even if my mind keeps telling me this negative belief is true, I am committed to taking bold action toward finishing my dissertation and willing to learn from mistakes I make along the way.

Negative Belief: I can't stand working on my dissertation.
Rational Coping Statement: I often have the thought, "I can't stand working on my dissertation." I also frequently have the feeling and experience that working on my dissertation is tedious, boring, and anxiety-provoking. Buying these thoughts and my feelings at face value contributes to procrastination and avoidance of my dissertation work. The more I procrastinate, the harder it seems to get started, and I begin to feel completely overwhelmed by the project. If I am honest with myself, these outcomes are worse than the discomfort of being bored and sitting down to work on my dissertation. The longer I put off my dissertation, the worse I feel about it and the more likely I am to put it off even more. I can work on my dissertation even if I am bored, uncomfortable, or having the thought that I can't stand working on my dissertation.

Negative Belief: I should have been able to create a strong theoretical framework by now. Maybe this is sign that I am not cut out to earn a PhD.
Rational Coping Statement: In reality, developing a strong theoretical framework takes time even for talented students. Struggling to theorize in the process of developing a dissertation study does not mean I am not capable of doing doctoral level work. All researchers bump up against intellectual challenges while conducting research. This struggle is a normal part of being a researcher and does not mean they are incompetent or incapable. When I demand that I should have been able to figure out a theoretical framework by now, I make myself panic. Thus, it becomes difficult to slow down, take my time, and be thoughtful so I can figure out the issues. I am willing to struggle, be uncomfortable, and stay engaged while I work through this intellectual hurdle.

Negative belief: I do not have enough time to make progress on my dissertation.
Rational Coping Statement: My mind keeps telling me that I do not have enough time to make progress on my dissertation. When I accept my belief as a belief instead of the truth, I can consider that I do have other options such as honestly looking at my schedule and carefully planning my week so I can make better use of time. I recognize that I can have this belief in my mind and find a way to manage my schedule and work on my dissertation.

CREATE YOUR OWN RATIONAL COPING STATEMENTS

Take some time to construct a rational coping statement for yourself (see Exercise 3.2). Write down one of your own negative beliefs and then craft a statement that reflects a more accepting and flexible way of thinking. Practice cognitive defusion by writing statements that reflect observations of your thoughts, feelings, and so forth (e.g., "My mind is telling me . . ." or "I am having the feeling/thought that . . .") and acknowledge how their presence does not need to interfere with taking action. You may also want to consider how you can reflect a growth mind-set in the statement.

Ellis and MacLaren (1998) pointed out that creating effective rational, coping statements requires practice. In particular, practice these skills when

EXERCISE 3.2

Create a Rational Coping Statement

Write down a negative belief and use the above guidelines to craft a rational coping statement. Take your time and do not worry about writing a perfect statement. You may want to write and revise your rational coping statement over time.

Negative Belief: _____

Rational Coping Statement:

_____

_____

_____

_____

_____

_____

_____

you are not under a high degree of stress. When you are under stress, you are more vulnerable to cognitive fusion and getting caught in thinking traps. You may want to keep a journal or a document on your computer where you engage in defusion and reading and creating rational coping statements for a few minutes daily. Cognitive defusion and rational coping statements are skills that, with practice, can become second nature to you and ultimately free you to make progress on your dissertation.

In addition to writing out rational coping statements, you may find it helpful to record the positive thoughts and beliefs you naturally have about yourself, your dissertation, and being a doctoral student. If, for example, you are proud of your accomplishments or what you are learning, take some time to write down your positive thoughts. Reviewing this list may also help you maintain a more positive outlook.

Strategy 5: Take Bold Action Consistent With Your Values

In chapter 1, you had the chance to identify your own personal values. By values, I mean the qualities you believe are important to demonstrate in your life. Values are about the way you live your life and the direction you take (Hayes & Smith, 2005). As a graduate student, you are seeking more than a doctoral degree, you are seeking to demonstrate certain qualities of being human through action and the way you live your life. I encourage you to revisit your answers to the questions in chapter 1 about values (see Exercise 1.3). If you did not complete the exercise, now would be a good time to do so. Consider the questions again and see if there is anything you would like to change or add to your list of values.

Earlier in this chapter, I defined active acceptance as being willing to fully and courageously experience whatever life throws at you. This acceptance is in the service of being in the moment with unwanted experiences instead of reacting to them through behavior that is designed to avoid or escape them. Thus, you are able to take action consistent with your values and your values-driven goals even in the presence of unwanted experiences. Having clear value directions to follow and to guide you is important especially when you are faced with thinking, feeling, and behaving traps that threaten to derail you from taking action. For example, if you are clear that you value creativity and learning, these values communicate a direction for you to follow even when self-doubt and anxiety show up at your door. You have a choice. You can avoid your thoughts and feelings or you can courageously move forward and step on the pathway that is lighted by your values of learning and creativity.

SOME THOUGHTS ON VALUES

Before I discuss setting goals and taking bold action in line with your values, I want to make a few important points about values and values-based living. First, you have values even if you do not think you do. Sometimes students worry that they do not have values because they have been avoiding their dissertation, being apathetic, or focusing only on performing well. They tell me they obviously do not value learning, academic achievement, productivity, accomplishment, or other important values. These students are confusing values with goals. Goals are things you can achieve living life according to your values. Completing your dissertation is a concrete, achievable goal. Values are never achieved. Rather, they give you a direction in which to live your life. Just because you may not have been meaningfully engaged in your dissertation or the process of learning does not mean values are absent in your life. The fact that you have been struggling and are still seeking a way to finish this project tells me that you do value something. You actually care about this project and its completion. I highly doubt you decided to get a doctoral degree because you had nothing better to do with your time. So I encourage you to look again. What do you care about? What does completing this project and earning this degree mean to you? What qualities will it enable you to demonstrate?

Second, values are not in the future but lived out in the present (Hayes & Smith, 2005). Taking bold action is about the choices you make in the moment in a specific situation. For example, do you choose to express your values of contribution and excellence in the moment or do you respond to apathy, fear, and low frustration tolerance with nonacceptance and avoidance? You are the only person who can make that choice.

It is not right or wrong which choice you make, but choosing valued action will lead to a life more fully lived and a dissertation that is done.

Third, valued living is not necessarily easy. If it were easy, I would not be writing about this strategy. It takes integrity, commitment, and courage to live according to your values. This way of living means you, not your thoughts and feelings, are in charge of where you go (Hayes & Smith, 2005).

Fourth, no human being is always living according to his or her values (Hayes & Smith, 2005). You are not failing when you act inconsistent with your values, so don't judge yourself when you are not living according to them. So often students beat themselves up believing they are bad or wrong if their behavior is not in alignment with their values. They, like almost all human beings, tend to evaluate themselves in an all-or-nothing manner. I often hear people describe their behavior using terms such as good–bad, success–failure, productive–unproductive, or right–wrong. I think this is a rather cruel metric to use when you are evaluating yourself. As a consequence, students feel they need to make big, sweeping changes to their behavior to make themselves good, successful, productive, or right. It is usually unrealistic to expect yourself to make big changes all at once. For example, a plan to lose weight consisting of working out an hour every day and ending all consumption of desserts, processed foods, alcohol, and so on, usually backfires because it is too much change all at once. The plan does not allow any flexibility or small changes and adjustments to your lifestyle over time.

Instead of using an all-or-nothing metric, I encourage my clients to evaluate themselves in a different way. Ask yourself, "Am I moving toward or away from my values?" In this way you can evaluate your progress in a kinder, gentler way and consider what small adjustments you can make to move your behavior back in the direction of your values. As an illustration of my point, take a moment right now and stand on one foot. See if you can achieve complete balance (by complete balance I mean you are completely still with absolutely no movement in your foot, leg, or torso). Notice that no matter how intensely you focus on achieving balance, you cannot actually achieve it. You can probably become relatively centered standing on one foot but you need to keep making small adjustments to your body to be able to maintain a sense of balance. This exercise is a lot like living a values-directed life. Living in alignment with your values always requires adjustment. You need to keep making contact with your values over and over again and choosing behavior (small steps will do) toward those values. Sometimes you get out of balance and lean a little too much in one direction (e.g., when you begin to avoid thoughts and feelings) and need to reorient yourself around your values. Do not be hard on yourself for moving away from your values. It happens to everyone. Rather, think of it as an opportunity to learn how you can move in the direction of your values.

GOALS

You obviously have the goal of finishing your dissertation. In chapters 4 and 5 you will learn a systematic, structured approach to breaking down the larger goal of finishing your dissertation into practical, obtainable goals. This structured approach will help you clarify each step you need to take on the path to finishing your dissertation. The dissertation goals you set for yourself are not just about components of the dissertation process, such as writing, reading literature, collecting data, or conducting analysis. The goals represent your values such as the desire to learn, demonstrate integrity, accomplish, achieve, create, and contribute. As you are setting and striving to meet dissertation goals, I encourage you to be conscious of not only your goals and how you can achieve them but also what values the goals represent. In this way, when unwanted thoughts and feelings show up, you have clarity about the direction you want to move in. You as a human being can move in the direction of your goals even if your thoughts and feelings protest. You can hear the protest, thank the protest for sharing its opinion while allowing the protest to exist, and reach out toward the goals you have created for yourself.

The goals you will learn to create in the next two chapters will give you the chance to practice building new patterns of effective behavior. Moving in a valued direction will help serve your long-term interests of making progress instead of the short-term interests of escaping and avoiding painful or difficult private experiences. I encourage you to think of each day and each dissertation work session as opportunities to stretch yourself and your ability to do what will make a difference toward completing your dissertation even in the face of thoughts and feelings you have habitually avoided.

When you seek to attain goals and build new behavioral patterns, the behavior changes you make can lead to cognitive and emotional changes. For example, a client named Lisa was working toward a PhD in sociology. When I met her, she had been avoiding the analysis of her data for close to 6 months. When we talked in depth about the barriers she was experiencing, it became clear that she was thinking about her data in a limiting way. Lisa was using a qualitative methodology, and she had interviewed 32 community organizers around the United States. As she began analyzing the data, she determined that her study would be better if she has asked additional questions and conducted the interviews differently. She started telling herself,

> I should have amended the interview guide after the first few interviews. I should have asked better questions and done a better job probing for more information. My data are not good enough. What is the point of analyzing them?

Lisa assumed that her data were worthless, and she felt anxious and experienced stomachaches every time she contemplated analyzing her data. She coped by avoiding her analyses altogether.

I encouraged Lisa to be more accepting of her negative thoughts and fears and begin analyzing her data even while having unwanted private experiences. We discussed her commitment to community organizing and how her research was a way for her to demonstrate the values of community, commitment, making a difference, collaboration, peace, and social justice. Lisa spent some time visualizing herself acting in accordance with her values instead of in reaction to her fears and self-doubt. It took a lot of courage and reassurance, but Lisa was willing to change her behavior in the presence of challenging thoughts and feelings and begin analyzing her data. Within 2 weeks of being engaged in her data analysis, Lisa reported feeling optimistic about her data and her ability to write a meaningful dissertation. She actually began to believe her data contained important findings despite imperfections and that she would be able to make a contribution to her field of study.

Lisa's story offers an important lesson. Being able to have positive thoughts and feelings is not a prerequisite to being able to work on your dissertation. If you engage in behavior that is consistent with what you value, you may find that your negative thoughts and feelings diminish or even change for the better. Even if they do not change, you are still moving in the direction of finishing your dissertation. You have the choice to behave as if you have positive thoughts and feelings even if you do not. Many people are waiting until they feel motivated or inspired to change their behavior. If you wait to take action until you think and feel like it is a good, safe, or reasonable idea, you may wait a long time.

Finally, on the path to meeting your values-driven goals, I encourage you to hold an accepting, compassionate, and forgiving stance toward setbacks, barriers, and obstacles. How you evaluate a bout of procrastination, for example, will impact your ability to get back on your feet and move toward your goals and values. If you judge yourself and become nonaccepting of the thoughts and feelings that are driving procrastination, then the repertoire of behavior you can engage in becomes limited. If you can make room for the thoughts and feelings and connect with your values, then you are more likely to have the courage to return to your work. I recognize that taking these steps is not easy. But it is a workable pathway to the goal of finishing your dissertation and living a life aligned with your values.

Strategy 6: Therapy, Self-Help Books, and Coaching

The degree to which humans are hampered by negative thinking, behavior, and emotional patterns varies. Some people develop restricted, rigid beliefs and patterns of thinking, feeling, and behaving that have a profound impact on their psychological well-being, their relationships, and how they relate to and respond to the world (Ellis, 2001). In my experience, there are times when graduate students need help to gain freedom from these patterns. They may also have issues related to their family or personal history, unique biochemistry, and their ability to focus their attention and regulate their emotions and behavior that may influence their mental health and ability to successfully complete a doctoral dissertation. If it seems that you are entrenched in patterns that are seriously hindering you, I encourage you to seek professional help. Most universities have counseling centers that offer students psychotherapy and psychiatric services at little or no cost. Some counseling centers have special groups, specifically designed for graduate students that are focused on stress, anxiety, procrastination, or even on completing dissertations. The support and wisdom you can gain from psychotherapy or a support group can be immensely helpful at a time when it is easy to feel demoralized and isolated.

Other resources that you may find helpful are the books on changing beliefs and thinking patterns, overcoming procrastination or perfectionism, and strategies for writing and self-care, listed in the reference section of this book. You may also consider working with a dissertation coach. (There are a growing number of dissertation coaches around the country.) An important part of my work with many clients is to help them simultaneously change and accept patterns of thinking, feeling, and behaving. Yet, when I believe anxiety, depression, or some other serious issue is interfering with a student's progress (and ability to make use of our coaching relationship), I refer these clients for psychotherapy.

Moving on to Action

At this point, you have learned a lot about common thinking, feeling, and behaving traps and how you can free yourself from them. So, what is next? Well, it is time to do something with that freedom. It is time to take action and make progress on your dissertation. To facilitate your progress, I will teach you a structured, project-management approach to finishing your dissertation in chapters 4 and 5. You will learn to carefully plan and manage the work you need to do over time with a high level of specificity. A clear plan makes it easier for students to think and feel positively about their dissertation work and build a sense of momentum as they systematically complete one task after the other. In chapter 4, you will learn how to break down the larger goal of completing your dissertation into weekly goals by creating a timeline for carrying out your dissertation. In chapter 5, you will learn how to break down your weekly goals into realistic daily action plans. My hope is that the use of timelines and action plans will be an important way to help you take bold action to move your dissertation forward and bring this important project to completion.

Devising Timelines
Avoiding a Breakdown by Breaking it Down

4

C ompleting a dissertation is admittedly no small task. It requires sustained effort and stamina over a long period of time. Many students find it easy to feel overwhelmed by the enormity of a dissertation project and to be uncertain of how to approach the process. Typical students I encounter have developed one or more of the following habits in response to the challenge of doing a dissertation:

1. Consistently instructing themselves to "work on my dissertation" or complete another large, ambiguously defined goal with no real sense of what that instruction means

2. Making long to-do lists of dissertation-related activities and planning to complete those activities in an unrealistic time frame

3. Working on big tasks such as writing a chapter, collecting data, or writing a discussion section with no real specific sense of what they need to do in a given day or week

4. Planning stretches of time such as "working all weekend" to work on their dissertation with no clear plan of what to do and how to approach their work during that period

5. Creating goals without being aware of the values their goals represent

Regardless of whether those habits sound familiar to you, I find that most graduate students benefit from learning a more structured approach to completing a dissertation. By structured, I mean breaking the larger goal of completing a dissertation into much smaller goals and connecting the smaller goals to realistic time frames. You have likely heard this advice from friends and faculty members. Many books offering advice on procrastination recommend using some version of task analysis, a process of breaking down large tasks into smaller tasks to make it easier to complete them. This is good advice. Yet the advice is limited in that insufficient detail is provided to help students understand what breaking down their dissertation goals would actually look like.

When I lead dissertation workshops, I always give students an important piece of information that seems to be missing from doctoral education. That information is that being a graduate student means that you need to wear two hats. One hat is that of the person who does the actual work necessary to earn a PhD. The second and often unrecognized hat is that of the project manager who actively manages his or her own energy and structures the work of completing a dissertation in the context of other responsibilities. This chapter and chapter 5 center on teaching you ways to structure your dissertation and more fully step into the role of project manager.

As I mentioned in chapter 1, doctoral students often approach completing a dissertation a bit like the challenge of climbing Mount Everest. They tell themselves that they need to complete a very large dissertation task, such as writing a literature review, conducting their data analysis, or even worse, working on their dissertation in a global sense. Large dissertation goals such as these are a bit like saying, "I am going to climb Mount Everest without knowing the best approach or path to take or how much is reasonable to climb in a day." Being a project manager and creating structure is fundamentally about breaking down the Mount Everest of your dissertation into a series of hills. It will still take effort, hard work, and at times courage to climb those "dissertation hills." Yet when you aim to do a smaller piece of your dissertation, such as writing a draft of a subsection of your literature review, reading several specific articles, or conducting a subset of analyses, you increase the odds of making tangible progress. The structured approach reviewed in this chapter and chapter 5 is designed to help you increase your productivity and motivation while decreasing procrastination and the feeling of being overwhelmed.

The structured approach I use as a dissertation coach involves two main parts: (a) timelines to plan the overall process of completing your dissertation and (b) action plans that detail daily goals over a 1-week period. Timelines are described in this chapter and action plans in chapter 5. Timelines and action plans work in tandem to help you maintain an overall sense of what you need to accomplish in both the long and the short term to meet your goals.

Benefits of Timelines

Writing a timeline that has realistic estimates (as realistic as possible) of how long various dissertation tasks will take to complete has a number of benefits. First, creating a timeline is about breaking down your dissertation into much smaller goals that are easier to approach and that you believe you can complete. The use of a timeline is a way of creating smaller goals you can actually imagine completing in 1 week or less. Smaller goals generally require less motivation and willpower to complete, thereby decreasing procrastination. Second, a well-crafted timeline can help you focus and direct your energy toward completing specific, tangible goals each week. In this way, timelines become an important energy-management tool to help you harness and focus your energy to increase productivity and make concrete progress. Third, the timeline allows you to have a greater sense of control over the dissertation process. The presence of the timeline can help ease some of your worries and fears about completing the entire project because you can more clearly see how you will complete your dissertation step by step. Fourth, the timeline helps you better see the relative importance of completing short-term goals, by showing the consequences of failing to complete those upcoming goals. In most academic departments, there are no interim deadlines or consequences if you do not complete a dissertation goal such as writing a portion of a chapter or conducting a set of analyses by a certain date. Having a timeline in place can help you feel more accountable to meet interim goals and improve your overall progress. Fifth, the timeline can be used to break down and plan other important academic endeavors, such as coursework or publication writing, or even other major life events or projects that are happening concurrent with your dissertation. Finally, creating a timeline can be a way for you to clarify the values that reaching your goals will allow you to demonstrate. In this way, your timeline and the milestones it comprises give you a way to define a direction to guide your behavior so that it is consistent with your values.

Creating Timelines

Most doctoral students I meet have created a dissertation timeline on at least one occasion. Some graduate programs even require students to submit a timeline for completing their dissertations at the time they propose or if they need to file for an extension for more time to complete their dissertation. If you have ever made a timeline, was it helpful?

Were you able to follow it? Were your goals attainable? Did you look at it on a regular basis, or did you forget about it or ignore it once you got off track? Did you find the timeline sitting at the bottom of a pile of paper months after you made it?

I have found that many doctoral students who make a dissertation timeline seldom use it in a meaningful way. Instead of revising the timeline on a regular basis, it is common for graduate students to set it aside as soon as they fall behind or never look at it again after they initially make the plan. Often students are uncertain how to create a sound work plan for major academic projects. Following the four guidelines presented next will help you make effective and realistic timelines.

GUIDELINE 1: CREATE CLEAR, SPECIFIC DISSERTATION MILESTONES

The first guideline to follow in making effective timelines is to break down larger dissertation goals into smaller goals you can accomplish in a relatively short time frame. I generally define a dissertation milestone as a specific, discrete goal with a clear beginning and end that you can accomplish in 1 week or less. Common examples are writing a rough first draft of a subsection of a chapter, collecting a portion of data, conducting a specific set of analyses, or planning to read several chapters in a book. You might break down the goals of writing your methodology chapter into writing the subsections of your study participant section, procedure, measures section, and proposed analyses. Goals such as "review the literature," "write chapter 2," or "analyze data" are not specific or small enough for most students. When a goal is too large, it is usually unclear where to direct your energy and begin your work in a given work session. The act of making specific milestones with a clear beginning and end helps you focus your energy on the task at hand instead of using your energy to figure out what to do first. The example timelines provided later in this chapter will help you develop a better sense of what dissertation milestones look like.

GUIDELINE 2: ASSIGN YOUR MILESTONES TO SPECIFIC DATES

In addition to being specific, I emphasize assigning milestones to specific dates so you know when you need to complete each milestone. I recommend that you space your timeline milestones 1 week apart. Timeline milestones can be spaced apart 2 weeks or more as you plan your timeline further into the future (beyond the upcoming few weeks of your plan) and have a less precise sense of what you will need to do when. In general, I find that creating milestones that are due on a weekly basis is better for two reasons. First, it is more likely that you will define dissertation goals in a way that is achievable in that time frame if you know you only have 1 week to complete them. Second, weekly milestones decrease the odds of procrastination. In my experience, when students have 2 weeks or longer to complete a task, they tell themselves at the beginning of the first week, "I have 2 weeks, I can do this later." The next thing they know, an entire week has gone by and they have not done any work toward completing the milestone. When a goal is pared down to something that can be accomplished in a week, students often feel greater urgency to work on the goal because they only have 7 days in which to accomplish it. Another benefit of weekly goals is that if you finish ahead of the timeline, you can use the remaining time to relax, celebrate, and have fun. In this way, you receive positive reinforcement after completing a manageable task that motivates you to stick to your plan in the coming week.

Usually, I encourage students to pick a day of the week when their weekly milestones are due (Sunday is most popular) and create a written plan that lists milestones under those dates. Exhibit 4.1 provides an example of what milestones in a timeline might look like. These milestones are from a larger dissertation timeline of a nursing doctoral student named Scott. Scott was at a point where he was writing the results chapter of a quantitative study on factors that contributed to quality of

---

EXHIBIT 4.1

Examples of Milestones

By August 30
- Written descriptive statistics section of results.
- Written first regression model and output.
- Sent first regression write-up to my advisor for review to make sure I am writing regression according to her standards.
- Written a rough outline of the rest of the results section.
- Met with advisor (toward end of week) to discuss first regression write-up.

By September 6
- Written data analysis sections in results.
- Revised first regression write-up based on advisor's feedback.
- Written up regression model 2.
- Written up regression model 3.

By September 13
- Written regression model 4.
- Written regression model 5.
- Written regression model 6.
- Revised write-ups of all six regressions.
- Polished methods section and add alpha levels to measures section.
- Sent methods and all six regression write-ups to advisor for review.

life and physical well-being among nursing home residents. The listed milestones are goals he planned to accomplish by three consecutive Sundays in August and September. Under each of the three dates, he has listed the specific tasks he plans to accomplish by the particular date. Each milestone is clear and specific and something he can accomplish in 1 week or less. You will notice in Scott's timeline that he wrote his milestones in the past tense. Some of my clients write them this way to serve as a reminder that the goals need to be completed by the date under which they are listed. The tense you use for your milestones (past or present) is up to you.

GUIDELINE 3: MAKE A REALISTIC TIMELINE

When you create a timeline, I strongly encourage you to make it as realistic as possible. Often students look out at the months or years ahead—and what it will take to complete their dissertation—and begin to feel anxious. So they make a timeline that emphasizes soothing their anxiety over being honest about how long their work will take. When students construct a dissertation timeline, there is frequently a little voice in their heads telling them that the plan they are making is unrealistic. That little voice often says things like, "you can't do all of that work in 1 week" or "you should give yourself more time," but when anxiety abounds, that voice is ignored.

If the amount of work planned in your timeline is not realistic, then you are setting yourself up to be unable to stick to your plan (and likely to feel bad about failing to meet your work goals). Do your best to avoid using your timeline as an anxiety-management tool that gives you a temporary, albeit false, sense of control over how you will get your work done.

So how do you know what is realistic? The honest answer is that it is hard to know. If your gut instinct is that what you are planning to do is unrealistic, then I advise you to rethink your timeline and lower your expectations. The guideline I give graduate students is to think of making timelines as walking the line between being realistic about what they can accomplish and challenging themselves to work hard. I encourage you to emphasize being realistic a little more than challenging yourself, especially when you are learning to use the structured approach described here. I have seen that many students make unrealistic work plans and to do lists or do not plan at all. Thus, they do not know how to realistically estimate what they can accomplish in a given period. Allow yourself several weeks (or as long as you need) to use the timeline structure to develop better instincts about what is realistic to accomplish in a given week. In the beginning, you may need to revise your plan a good deal, but if you are consistent about creating and revising your timeline you will develop a better ability make good estimates of what you can accomplish. If being realistic is a struggle for you, then consider getting a reality check from another person who can help you be more honest about what you can accomplish on a weekly basis.

GUIDELINE 4: MAINTAIN YOUR TIMELINE IN AN ELECTRONIC FORM

When it comes to the actual construction of a dissertation timeline, I encourage you to create an electronic version of your timeline in a word processing or database software such as Microsoft Word or Microsoft Excel. I find that handwritten timelines do not work well for students, as they are hard to revise. An electronic version of your timeline allows you to easily revise it, print multiple copies, and e-mail it to others such as your dissertation chairperson or peers in a dissertation support group. Keep your timeline simple, so that it is easy to create, modify, and maintain over time.

Making Timelines

In general, there are three main stages of completing a dissertation: (a) developing a sound dissertation topic (including research questions), (b) writing a dissertation proposal, and (c) carrying out and completing the dissertation study. It is usually better to make a timeline for each stage separately rather than trying to make one timeline for the duration of the dissertation process from start to finish. For example, it would not be possible to make a timeline for writing the proposal or completing the study if you do not have a well-developed research topic. Once you have a sound dissertation topic, you could create a timeline for the proposal and carrying out the actual dissertation study all at one time. Yet I recommend waiting to make a timeline for carrying out and completing your dissertation until you have successfully proposed your dissertation. I make this recommendation because: (a) until you know precisely what your study will entail post-defense, it is hard to plan beyond the proposal phase; and (b) students' dissertation proposals often require modification that is based on the input of their dissertation committee. Therefore, it makes more sense to wait to create a timeline for completing your dissertation until you know what you will be doing and what your committee expects of you.

Before we review the sample timelines in this chapter, it is important to note that every student's dissertation experience is different. When you review the sample timelines, I encourage you to avoid using them as indicators of how long it "should" take you to complete various dissertation tasks. For example, the time it takes to analyze data in dissertations with an experimental design varies greatly depending on the unique characteristics of the particular dissertation study. Also, you cannot necessarily expect your chairperson to give you feedback in the same time frame, as you will see in the sample timelines. The length of time various dissertation activities take will vary depending on factors such as your field of study, previous knowledge and experience with the dissertation topic, ease of access to study participants, methodology, and the amount of feedback your dissertation chairperson provides. My advice, therefore, is to use the example timelines in this chapter as a guideline to help you make your own dissertation plan. At the same time, I encourage you to avoid comparing yourself and your dissertation trajectory with the examples in a way that makes you feel inferior or inadequate. Remember, there is a unique context behind the sample timelines in this chapter that is different from your own.

PREPARING TO MAKE A TIMELINE

Before you sit down to make a timeline, there is preparatory work you can do to make the process easier. You will benefit from creating a pre-timeline inventory. This inventory is a list of all the tasks you can think of that you need to complete to develop a topic, write your proposal, or carry out and write the final dissertation. This pre-timeline inventory will be less specific if you are developing a topic or if you are in the early stage of writing your proposal, but it is worth making nonetheless. It is best to make this pre-timeline inventory as detailed as possible, breaking down literature into lists of books and specific content areas of articles that you will need to read, sections you think you will write (including what has been written to date and what needs revision), and listing any work related to recruiting study participants; gathering, entering, cleaning, and analyzing data; and any other goals you will need to complete. Make sure you note tasks such as selecting committee members, development or selection of measures, library research on particular topics, obtaining source material, and applying for human participants' approval, as these issues are relevant.

Of course, it is not possible to foresee everything that you will need to do to complete a particular stage of your dissertation. You do not need to know everything ahead of time. Just make your inventory as complete as possible and trust that when you obtain more information about what you will need to do, you will revise your timeline and incorporate new tasks into your plan. Exhibit 4.2 is an example of a pre-timeline inventory from a student named Janet, who was conducting a qualitative study that examined how adolescent girls resisted gender stereotypes. When she made this inventory, she had already proposed her dissertation and collected part of her interview data. The remaining

EXHIBIT 4.2

Janet's Dissertation Inventory

Data Collection
- Recruit 7 additional study participants.
- Interview 7 additional study participants.
- Transcribe 7 new interviews.

Finish Methods Chapter
- Analyze descriptive statistics.
- Revise participants section including descriptive statistics.
- Update measures and procedures section as needed.
- Write section describing grounded theory as it pertains to my study.
- Write description of how qualitative data analyses were conducted.

Data Analysis
- Read all 14 transcripts at least two times, writing down initial codes–themes and ideas.
- Keep running list of ideas for results and discussion chapters as I read and code data.
- Meet with my advisor, review initial codes, and discuss next steps for analysis.

Write Results Chapter[a]
- Not enough information on how I will write up results.

Write Discussion Chapter[b]
- Summary of results.
- Theoretical integration.
- Discuss research by Gilligan, Brown, Spinazzoa, Wilson, Stocking, and others as they pertain to my work.
- Practical implications.
- Limitations–future research.

Other Work
- Update appendices and references.
- Submit entire dissertation to chairperson for feedback (probably twice) and integrate feedback.
- Format dissertation according to university guidelines.
- Schedule dissertation defense (& reserve a room).
- Submit dissertation to my committee for final defense.
- Defend dissertation.

[a]At the time Janet made the inventory she did not have enough information about how she would conduct her qualitative analyses or write up her results. Thus, we planned to revise her timeline again once she had a better sense of her analysis strategy and findings. [b]Here Janet is guessing as to what she thinks she will write for her discussion chapter. Again, we planned to revise her timeline as she obtains more information.

work included interviewing 7 additional study participants, analyzing her data, updating her method chapter, and writing her results and discussion chapters. At the point she made this inventory, it was not apparent how she would carry out every aspect of her dissertation so she provided as much information as she had.

Janet used this initial inventory to create a timeline by connecting the various goals in the inventory to specific dates. In the timeline, she reminded herself to revise the plan once she had more information about her data analysis, results, and discussion chapters.

"DEVELOP A TOPIC" TIMELINE

The stage of developing a dissertation topic and research questions is usually the most challenging stage to make a timeline for, because these tasks usually have more than one clear course of action. Timelines for developing a topic require the most monitoring and ongoing revision. As your dissertation topic can change from week to week (and even day to day), the corresponding tasks you need to complete will also change. Thus, during the "develop a topic" phase of your dissertation be prepared to revise your timeline on a frequent basis. So, what would a timeline for developing a dissertation topic look like? The answer obviously varies considerably depending on factors such as your field of study, whether you have a narrowed down an area of research, access to existing data, and the degree of faculty involvement in your dissertation. Nonetheless, in Exhibit 4.3 I offer an example of what a "develop a topic" timeline can look like.

The timeline in Exhibit 4.3 is from a student I will refer to as David. David is a doctoral student in community psychology who was considering developing a study about mentoring relationships among minority youth. He became interested in this topic as a result of his experience mentoring two adolescent males through a Big Brother program. Yet he was only moderately familiar with the existing literature on mentoring relationships and had no specific research questions or study design in mind. The timeline he created helped him plot an initial course of action to become more familiar with the literature and develop a viable dissertation study.

David's plan helped him be systematic in his approach to identifying a topic and research questions for his study. It allowed him to have a clear course of action each week so that he was not just reading literature or thinking about research ideas with no real sense of direction. What you will notice in this timeline is that David is engaged consistently in five main activities: (a) reading and identifying relevant research studies and literature, (b) taking notes and giving careful thought to what he is reading, (c) outlining, (d) writing, and (e) meeting his advisor (you may also want to meet with other faculty members and even peers). All of these activities are potentially useful as you develop a topic. As you work on creating a timeline for developing a topic, think about these five activities and what other activities would help you in your own quest to develop a sound dissertation topic and research questions.

Choose a topic you will care about and enjoy. Having done this, it will be easier for you to focus on having your dissertation experience be about demonstrating your values and learning instead of performing and proving yourself. At the same time, recognize that your dissertation will not be the definitive work completed in your research area. In fact, it may just be a study that slightly expands on previous work. That is

EXHIBIT 4.3

David's "Develop a Topic" Timeline

By January 13
- Read at least half of *Handbook on Youth Mentoring.*
- Take notes on reading—note areas of interest, potential areas of focus for a dissertation study, other research cited in the handbook to obtain.
- Start a running outline of ideas for problem statement.

By January 20
- Read remaining half of *Handbook on Youth Mentoring.*
- Take notes on reading—note areas of interest, potential areas of focus for a dissertation study, other research cited in the handbook to obtain.
- Add to outline for problem statement and note any ideas on research questions.

By January 27
- Read special issue of *American Journal of Community Psychology* on youth-mentoring relationships.
- Take notes on reading—note areas of interest, potential areas of focus for a dissertation study, other research cited in the journal to obtain.
- Add to outline for problem statement and note any ideas on research questions
- Set up a meeting with my advisor for next week.

By February 3
- Read special issue of *Journal of Primary Prevention* on youth-mentoring relationships.
- Take notes on reading—note areas of interest, potential areas of focus for a dissertation study, other research cited in the journal to note any ideas on research questions.
- Add to outline for problem statement.
- Meet with my advisor to discuss my ideas and observations so far (later in week).

By February 10
- Review articles to date.
- Note what questions I have; what seems unanswered by the literature.
- Identify methodological issues with past research.
- Note areas for future research noted in previous research.
- Note what interests me the most; what I want to know about.
- Write problem statement and research questions.
- Send problem statement and research questions to my advisor.

By February 17
- Meet with my advisor to discuss my problem statement and research questions.
- Make a plan of future work to do based on meeting with my advisor.

okay. Your dissertation is about demonstrating your competence as a researcher, learning, expanding your research skills, and earning a degree, not about completing a magnum opus. Also, make sure you pick a topic with a narrow enough focus that you can earn your degree in a reasonable time frame. Most important, you need your advisor or dissertation chairperson (and eventually your committee) to support your dissertation topic. Your chairperson and committee will have the ultimate say in whether your dissertation merits a doctoral degree. Thus, it is critical that they buy in to your topic and believe it is suitable for a student's dissertation study. Make sure you are open to your advisor's feedback as you develop your dissertation topic. You may want to ask your advisor to recommend several dissertations from your department that he or she views as good examples. Then you will be able to obtain a better sense of his or her expectations of a dissertation and what he or she considers to be an acceptable study.

The key to creating timelines for selecting a topic is to regularly monitor and review the timelines. Because this phase is not clear-cut, your work in any week or on any day may take you in a direction you did not plan or even lead to a dead end. For example, you may discover that the study you would like to do has already been done (although it is possible that there is a variation of the study that is worth conducting). It is also possible that a discussion with your advisor about the focus of your dissertation or lack of access to data, source material, or study participants may change the direction of your dissertation, making your timeline obsolete. I encourage you to continually take the time to structure this phase of the dissertation even if it means that you are only planning 1 week at a time. In my experience, making consistent progress in the quest to select a dissertation topic and identify a clear research focus is made easier when students have a clear, written course of action.

PROPOSAL TIMELINES

Once you have developed a sound dissertation topic and your chairperson has agreed that your topic is suitable, it is time to write a dissertation proposal. Your proposal is a document that communicates clearly to your committee what you plan to study and how you plan to carry out that study. In your written proposal, you must review pertinent literature, make a case for your study or argument, explain your research methodology, and adequately describe how you will analyze your data (if data are a part of your study). After you have developed your topic and research focus, you will be ready to create a timeline for writing your dissertation proposal.

The next timeline (Exhibit 4.4) is loosely based on an actual plan for a student I will refer to as Samantha. Samantha was enrolled in a clinical psychology doctoral program. Her dissertation study examined the influence of early maternal depression and parenting practices, such as parental monitoring, on later adolescent mental health and sexual risk taking among a sample of low-income, urban African American youth. At the time we made her timeline, she was planning to apply for a predoctoral clinical internship. To earn a doctorate in clinical psychology, it is required that students complete a yearlong internship providing clinical services, usually in a hospital or mental health setting. Internship applications are generally due in the fall, and interviews for internships occur in December and January. Samantha's graduate program had a requirement that to be allowed to go through the interview

EXHIBIT 4.4

Samantha's Timeline to Complete Her Dissertation Proposal

By June 26
- Research questions and measures given to advisor.
- Created very rough outline of literature review (determine main substantive areas to be covered)—modify timeline once I determine these areas.
- Set up a meeting with my advisor for next week.

By July 3
- Institutional Review Board process and potential committee members discussed with advisor.
- Feedback on research questions received from advisor.
- Created draft of model to be tested.
- Draft of purpose of study written.

By July 10
- Obtained articles on maternal depression and childhood–adolescent depression and developmental trajectories of adolescent depression (early in week).
- Read articles on childhood–adolescent depression.
- Met with Dr. Caldwell (potential committee member) to discuss possibility of having her on my committee.
- Confirmed that Dr. Sutter will be on my dissertation committee.
- Revised model and purpose of study and gave to advisor for feedback.

By July 17
- Read articles on maternal depression.
- Draft of participant section of method written.
- Draft of measures section of method written.
- Outlined maternal depression and childhood–adolescent depression section.
- Asked Dr. Skolnick to be on my committee.
- Asked Dr. Garner to be on my committee.

By July 24
- Section written on relationship between maternal depression and childhood–adolescent depression.
- Committee established (e-mailed advisor to confirm committee members).
- Feedback on model and purpose of study received from advisor.
- Revised literature review written to date.

By September 11
- Written literature review section on relationship between depression and sexual risk taking (first draft).
- Met with Dr. Caldwell to discuss structural equation modeling–regression models as they relate to my study.
- Full draft of participants, measures and procedure revised and completed.
- Read articles on peer influence and HIV risk–sexual risk taking.
- Outlined section on peer influence and HIV risk–sexual risk taking.

By September 18
- Outlined section on peer factors and HIV risk.
- Written literature review section on peer factors and HIV risk written (first draft).
- Integrated all of the sections of the literature review written to date—make sure purpose of study and research questions are written as part of the literature review.
- Meeting held with advisor to review proposed analyses.
- Revised literature review written to date.

By October 30
- Feedback received from advisor on proposal.

(continued)

EXHIBIT 4.4 (*Continued*)

- Feedback received from Dr. Caldwell.
- Made inventory of changes to make to proposal based on feedback from advisor and Dr. Caldwell.

By November 13 (2-week interval to allow herself time to enter final round of feedback on her proposal)[a]

- Feedback from advisor and Dr. Caldwell integrated.
- Met advisor (if I need to discuss any issues before submitting proposal to committee).
- Finalized proposal and sent to all five dissertation committee member.

By November 27

- Created PowerPoint presentation for proposal defense meeting.
- Met with advisor to discuss proposal meeting.
- Practice presentation for proposal defense.

By December 4

- Proposal defended.

[a]In Samantha's department it is the norm to submit proposals or final defense dissertation papers to the committee at least 2 weeks prior to the defense meeting. Find out the norms in your department to help you more accurately plan your timeline.

process and go on internship the following year, students must defend their dissertation proposal no later than the end of the semester (early December) they apply for internship.

In the month of June, Samantha and I made her first timeline to plan how she would write her dissertation proposal. Given her early December deadline, she only had 6 months available to complete her dissertation proposal. As a result you will notice that the pace of her proposal timeline is fairly quick. Also, you will see that we planned very short intervals of time for her to receive feedback from her advisor after submitting various drafts. Because of Samantha's time constraints, her advisor agreed to give her feedback on her proposal submissions in short intervals. You may not be able to secure such an agreement with your dissertation chairperson and may need to plan longer time intervals to wait for feedback. If your advisor takes weeks (or months) to give you feedback, then strive to plan other dissertation or academic work you can do while you are waiting.

The timeline was created in the month of June when she had a well-developed sense of her research questions and measures she would use in her study. Prior to making the timeline, she created a pre-timeline inventory of all of the major tasks she would need to accomplish to complete and defend her proposal. I worked with her to help her break down those tasks into milestones that we thought she could accomplish in 1 week or less. Once we made this list, we had the raw material to make her proposal timeline that connected the various milestone goals on the list to weekly intervals. Again, you will notice in Exhibit 4.4 Samantha used the past tense to describe the works she planned to complete by each weekly target, but feel free to use present tense as you make your timeline.

Samantha was able to follow this timeline very closely, and she successfully defended her proposal on December 9. Notice that her milestone goals are clear and specific and of a scope that is reasonable to accomplish in a week. She used the timeline to plan how she would identify and invite faculty members to join her dissertation committee as well as when she would meet her advisor and committee members to help her develop her proposal.

She planned ahead carefully so that she could complete the reading necessary to write a section the week before she intended to do the writing. Also, she built in time to draft various subsections of her literature review, method, and proposed analyses sections and then included sufficient time to revise those drafts. Samantha used her timeline to think through when she would give drafts to her advisor for review and anticipate when she would receive and integrate that feedback. For the sake of brevity, I provide portions of her overall timeline including the first 5 weeks of work, 2 weeks of work in the middle of her plan, and the last 5 weeks of her timeline.

Timelines to Complete Your Dissertation

Once you have successfully defended your dissertation proposal, you will then be ready to make a timeline to carry out and complete your dissertation study. Timelines for this stage of the dissertation vary considerably by student. Some students are able to create a timeline that takes them from the time they collect and analyze data all the way to the final completion of their dissertation and the dissertation defense. I find that students in the social sciences who plan to carry out a quantitative study are best able to create such as timeline. They have often carried out other quantitative studies and have a fairly good sense of the trajectory of completing their dissertation.

In contrast, students who conduct qualitative studies are not usually able to create a complete timeline through their dissertation defense, as the precise process of analyzing qualitative data is not always apparent until they are immersed in the analysis process. Timelines for qualitative dissertations tend to require more revision as the process of analyzing data is usually more involved and ambiguous. Other students, especially those in the humanities, may not be able to make a timeline beyond one chapter at a time as future chapters they write are dependent on the current chapter they are writing. In fact, at the outset of a chapter, you may only be able to create a timeline for 1 to 2 weeks, as you are brain-storming, free writing, and outlining to determine what you will write. Students in the hard sciences and some in the social sciences who run experiments may not be able to plan a timeline beyond the next experiment they need to run.

Regardless of how much you can or cannot plan due to the nature of your dissertation, I encourage you to make a timeline that provides you with a plan for as long as you can foresee. When you have more information about what you will need to do next, you can revise your timeline. What is most important is that you fully step into the role of project manager and manage the upcoming immediate work you need to do so you know when you need to do what.

Exhibit 4.5 is a timeline created by Janet, whose pre-timeline dissertation inventory was used as an example earlier in this chapter. Janet and I used that inventory to create the timeline in Exhibit 4.5 (although I only present part of her timeline here). This timeline begins at a point at which Janet was finishing study participant interviews and was soon to embark on the initial stages of analyzing her qualitative data. Because she had not collected all of her data, she did not have a precise sense of her data analysis strategy. Thus, this timeline includes her plan to develop an initial list of codes and work with her advisor to develop a more sophisticated data analysis strategy. At the point this timeline was made, it was not possible to plan how she would write her results or discussion chapters, as she did not have the results of her data analysis. Those stages of planning would be done at a later date.

Creating Short-Term and Vague Timelines

There are times when you cannot plan specific milestones beyond a short interval of time because you lack information about specific tasks. Perhaps you do not yet know how you will carry out your data analyses, what the results of an experiment will be, or what feedback you will receive from your chairperson. Thus, you will only be able to create specific milestones over the short term. In such a situation, plan specific milestones for as many weeks as you can. Then create a milestone that reminds you to revise your timeline once you know what the next steps will be. Let's say, for example, that you want to plan to write your literature review over an 8-week period but you do not have a well-developed sense of what the major sections of the literature review will be. This would make it difficult to create highly specific weekly milestones to break down the process of

EXHIBIT 4.5

Jane's Partial Timeline

By October 23
- Transcribe interviews 8, 9, and 10 (get help from my sister to complete).
- Interview last 2 study participants (11 and 12).

By October 30
- Transcribe interviews 11 and 12.
- Compile all descriptive data.
- Read interview 1 and 2 and create rough code–theme list or ideas for codes.

By November 6
- Catch up on any remaining transcription work that is incomplete.
- Run analyses on descriptive data.
- Read interview 3 and create rough code–theme list or ideas for codes.

By November 13
- Revise participant section of method and write up descriptive analyses.
- Revise procedures section of method (to capture what I actually did).
- Read interviews 4, 5, 6, and 7 and create code–theme list—revise existing codes list as I code these interviews.

By November 20
- Revise measures section to reflect the small changes I made to interview guide.
- Read interviews 8, 9, 10, 11, and 12 and create code–theme list—revise existing codes list as I code these interviews.

By November 27 (short week because of Thanksgiving)
- Type up code list and print out another copy of all 12 interviews to be ready for second round of coding next week.
- Write rough draft of section describing grounded theory as it pertains to my study (use Strauss and Corbin).

By December 4
- Set up meeting with my advisor to review data analysis and next steps.
- Carefully code interviews 1 to 6 a second time, revising and modifying the codes list along the way. Create new codes, collapse codes, and break codes apart as needed.

By December 11
- Carefully code interviews 7 to 12 a second time, revising and modifying the codes list along the way. Create new codes, collapse codes, and break codes apart as needed.
- Update data analysis description in method chapter to describe what I have done to date.
- Meet with my advisor to review data analysis and next steps (late in week).
- Revise timeline based on my meeting with my advisor to plan next steps for data analysis. Once analyses are done, plan outline results and discussion chapters and make a timeline for writing those chapters as well as finishing the data analysis section in the method, references, appendixes, etc.

writing the literature review. Yet it is still possible to make a timeline. Exhibit 4.6 shows what a timeline in such a situation might look like.

In this timeline, the milestones are vague because at the time the timeline was made, the student did not have enough information to make the milestones specific. The timeline as written reminds the student to specify those milestones by January 21 after she has outlined the literature review and has a better sense of its main content areas.

EXHIBIT 4.6

Short-Term or Vague Timeline

By January 14
- Brainstorm ideas and outline of literature review.

By January 21
- Talk with advisor about ideas for literature review.
- Revise outline.
- Write opening overview of my study.
- Revise timeline for next 4 weeks based on outline of study.

By January 28
- Draft one fourth of literature review (revise and make this milestone more specific based on content areas outlined the week leading up to January 21).

By February 4
- Draft one fourth of literature review (revise and make this milestone more specific based on content areas outlined the week leading up to January 21).

By February 11
- Draft one fourth of literature review (revise and make this milestone more specific based on content areas outlined the week leading up to January 21).

By February 18
- Draft one fourth of literature review (revise and make this milestone more specific based on content areas outlined the week leading up to January 21).

By February 24
- Read first draft of literature review and make a list of issues to be revised and concerns to be discussed with advisor (do this early in the week).
- Meet with advisor to discuss any issues–concerns about literature review (later in week).
- Create an inventory of literature review revisions to make based on meeting with my advisor.

By March 3
- Revise half of literature review.

By March 10
- Revise remaining half of literature review.
- Complete final read through and edit of literature review.
- Send literature review to my advisor for feedback.
- Brainstorm new dissertation goals and make a new timeline with Alison.

Once the outline is created, she can modify her milestones for January 28 through February 18 to reflect specific content areas to write about during each of the 4 weeks.

For most students, creating a timeline for the duration of time that they carry out their actual dissertation study will not be possible. For example, the actual research of many doctoral students consists of a series of experiments run in a laboratory. I have worked with students conducting psychological experiments with humans and biological or pharmacological experiments with animals, plants, and other organisms. In many situations, the results of a given experiment determine whether a student will need to run another experiment and even the specifics of how the next experiment is run. Thus, the student will need to continually create his or her dissertation timeline over time.

What I generally advise students to do in this situation is to make a timeline up through running their first experiment. Once that experiment is concluded, you can then make a short-term timeline for the next experiment, and the next, and so on until that phase of the dissertation is complete. Certainly, feel free to guess and create weekly milestones that give you an overall estimate of how long the experiment phase will take without being highly specific about what experiment you will be doing when. If you make a timeline this way, then you will just need to revise it frequently depending on the results of a given experiment. This advice also pertains to any student whose dissertation trajectory does not lend itself well to planning beyond a particular stage of the research process.

Don't Make Your Timeline Alone

Making a timeline for your dissertation can be challenging. It is often hard to make honest, realistic time estimates of how long various dissertation tasks will take. It is easy to rationalize to yourself that if you work very hard, you will be able to stick to what is actually an unrealistic plan. Students are often overly optimistic about how quickly they can write and how easy it will be to access study participants or research materials. Also, they forget to account for time spent waiting for feedback from their chairperson, committee members, or dissertation readers. The assistance of another person in making a timeline is especially important if you think anxiety will get the better of you when you try to estimate the time necessary for each stage of your dissertation. Another person is unlikely to be emotionally invested in your project and, can be more objective and help you better estimate how much work is realistic to accomplish in a given time frame. In addition, he or she can help you think through the various stages of your dissertation and how to break them down into smaller steps.

Fellow graduate students can be a good choice to help you construct timelines. Your graduate student peers understand the process in which you are engaged and what is expected of you as a student; you can reciprocate by helping fellow students make their own timelines and then hold each other accountable to your work plans. Making a timeline with your dissertation chairperson or another faculty member is also an option. I do caution you, however, that a faculty person's sense of how long it will take you to complete a major dissertation task may differ from what is realistic for a student. After many years of writing and conducting research, faculty are generally capable of carrying out various research tasks in a shorter time frame than are students. In general, I find that most faculty members are willing to review a student's timeline but prefer that students make timelines themselves. Friends and family members can also be helpful in making a timeline even if they know little about your dissertation. Whoever you choose, try to find someone who will help you take into account the other roles and responsibilities in your life when estimating how long your work will take. The bottom line is this: When it comes to making a timeline, especially when you are new to this approach, ask for help and avoid going it alone.

Align Your Timeline With Your Values

One way to increase the odds you will stick to your timeline is to be clear what values your goals represent. The more you pause and consider which values completing each goal represents, the easier it will be to take action consistent with your values even when unwanted experiences such as self-doubt, anxiety, and boredom occur. So, as you are creating your timeline, revisit the values list you created in Exercise 1.3. You may even want to record your values at the top of your timeline to help you stay present to them. If you find yourself resisting your timeline goals and actively avoiding your work, do your best to observe what unwanted thoughts and feelings you are actually avoiding and then strive to align your behavior with your values. You will likely need to realign yourself with your values again and again throughout your dissertation journey. Don't beat yourself up if you get off track (you inevitably will). Instead, have the courage to be compassionate toward yourself *and* move yourself in the direction of your values. Developing the ability to take such bold action is an important opportunity your dissertation experience offers you.

Timelines as a Source of Accountability

Once you have created a timeline, it can become an excellent tool to increase your sense of accountability. Many graduate students struggle to make consistent progress on their dissertation because there are few, if any, interim deadlines, and they do not feel accountable to anyone. A timeline in and of itself can provide students with deadlines and a sense of consequence for completing various dissertation goals. Sharing your timeline with others and asking them to hold you accountable for the weekly milestones are excellent ways to increase your productivity and motivation during the week. Knowing that someone will be asking you whether you have met your goals may increase the odds that you will complete the work.

Look for a person or group who will be willing to be both firm and supportive in their efforts to hold you accountable. I say "firm and supportive" because I have found a blend of these two qualities to best provide a tangible sense of accountability. Most students do well to feel that that their commitment to meeting timeline goals is being taken seriously by another person. At the same time, students want to feel supported and encouraged by the person holding them accountable. Praise for work completed and encouragement to revise their plan and get back on track when work is incomplete are important for many students.

Who can hold you accountable for the goals on your timeline? The answer to that question will vary by student. Graduate students in a dissertation support group can be very helpful in increasing accountability. Ask other students who are also working on their dissertations if they would like to create a dissertation support group and have accountability be a major purpose of the group. Meet on a regular basis (weekly to monthly depending on the needs and availability of group members) to review each member's timeline and action plan, check on each other's progress, revise timelines as necessary, and support each other to overcome barriers and challenges group members may be facing. The meeting can be held at school in an empty classroom, at each other's homes, or even local coffee shops or restaurants. When I was in graduate school, I participated in a dissertation support group that rotated around the homes of individual group members. The host was responsible for supplying food, and every member took a turn being the host. In lieu of a dissertation support group, you may find it helpful to find a dissertation buddy. A two-person partnership can be an excellent format to share dissertation timelines and increase accountability for both parties.

Your dissertation chairperson may also hold you accountable for meeting your timeline goals. Some students have chairpersons who are interested and willing to be highly involved in their student's dissertation process. Such advisors meet with their students on a regular basis and give feedback to their students in a very timely manner on drafts they have submitted. These types of advisors are often willing to hold you accountable for your goals. They may communicate that they expect you to turn in drafts as you have planned in your timeline and even check in with you when they see you in person or e-mail you about your planned work. After you have worked with your chairperson for some time, you will likely have a sense of whether or not he or she is willing to hold you to account for the work you plan to do. If you are not sure, it is okay to ask your chairperson directly. If your chairperson says no, then at least you know what to expect and you can look elsewhere.

Many faculty members do not see holding students accountable to meet interim dissertation goals as part of their role or responsibility as a dissertation chairperson. Whether your chairperson is willing to hold you accountable, it is generally a good idea to share your timeline with him or her. By sharing your timeline, you may learn important information that affects how you plan your weekly milestones. For example, your advisor may have a large grant application that is due, travel to an international conference, or a planned vacation that would affect his or her availability to give you feedback in the same time frame you have planned. Such information is obviously important in your own timeline planning process.

Friends and family members can also play a role in helping you feel accountable during the process of completing your dissertation. If you select friends or family members, take care to seek out people you believe will be both supportive and firm. You want friends and family members who take your commitment to finish your dissertation in a timely manner seriously and who can also be supportive when you are struggling. I suggest asking a friend or family member who is good at following through on meeting his or her own goals. Someone who procrastinates a lot or who has poor follow through may not provide a real sense of accountability. In general, I do not recommend relying on your spouse or significant other as a source of accountability. Intimate relationships are often challenging enough without adding this type of dynamic to them. If you think your spouse or significant other would be an excellent choice to create accountability, then go ahead and use this relationship for this purpose. If you have any doubt at all, then I recommend finding someone else. Whomever you choose to hold you accountable, make sure that you give that person or persons the revisions you make to your timeline regularly.

Revising Timelines

A dissertation timeline is effective only if you review it frequently and revise it as needed. Many students hope they can make a timeline on only one occasion, follow it perfectly, and never need to revise it. No matter how much you may have this desire, you *will* inevitably need to revise your timeline at some point. You will experience delays due to work that takes longer than you anticipated or issues outside your control (e.g., waiting for feedback from your advisor or Institutional Review Board approval, data collection issues, difficulty obtaining source material). Thus, your timeline will need revisions for one reason or another at multiple points in the time you work on your dissertation.

Students make two frequent mistakes with their timelines. One, they demand—irrationally—that their timeline must be followed absolutely perfectly. When they do not meet their demands, they tell themselves that they will never finish and label themselves as inadequate in some way. Consequently, they feel depressed, discouraged, demoralized, angry, or anxious. They conclude that the project management approach does not work, when actually it is their rigid demands that do not work. I encourage you to avoid using your timeline as a means to mentally beat yourself up. Strive to maintain a flexible and rational mind-set about your timeline, preferring to stick to it as planned while simultaneously recognizing that revisions are a necessary and acceptable part of carrying out your dissertation.

The second mistake students often make is failing to keep their timeline up to date when they get behind or it no longer accurately reflects the work they need to do. When your timeline is not current, the risk of procrastination and lack of productivity rises because you either do not know what you need to do or you become overwhelmed by trying to work without an accurate, structured plan. So I encourage you to make it a regular habit to revise your timeline even if the revision is minor. If you get behind, resist the temptation to move incomplete work goals into the next week without adjusting the overall plan. Certainly, there may be occasions when you can realistically finish incomplete work from a prior week plus the milestones planned for the current week all in 1 week. In general, however, I find that this is not a wise strategy, particularly when there is a great deal of work left over from a previous week. Remember that being a project manager means that you *actively* manage the process of completing a dissertation. Therefore, if you want to fully step into the role of dissertation project manager, then it is required that you modify your dissertation timeline whenever there is a need to do so. I encourage my clients to stop and assess their timeline once a week to determine whether it requires revision. Some of my clients write weekly reminders to themselves in their work plan to "revise timeline as needed." The time you spend revising your timeline will almost always save you time in the long run because a solid work plan helps you focus your energy on the work that needs to be done.

Breaking Down Your Timeline Goals

Once you have created a dissertation timeline, you will be ready to move on to the second part of the structured, project management approach. This part of the approach is about making detailed action plans to break down your weekly milestones goals and identify what you need to do on a day-to-day basis. Chapter 5 provides an overview of how to best create a sound action plan to increase your motivation and productivity and help you get to the dissertation finish line.

Creating Weekly Action Plans
Using Structure to Your Advantage

5

B y now, I hope you have a fairly good understanding of how to create your own dissertation timeline. The second element of the structured approach to help you manage your dissertation is the weekly action plan. As important as well-crafted timelines can be to help graduate students successfully complete their dissertations, I believe weekly action plans are equally important and at times more important. An action plan is a detailed plan that breaks down the upcoming weekly goals (milestones) of the timeline into smaller tasks that are realistic to complete on a daily basis. These actions are then assigned to specific days of the week so that you know what you need to do when. Breaking down your timeline milestones into actions helps you effectively translate your weekly goals into clear and achievable daily goals. Thus it is much easier to direct your energy to complete the daily tasks you have assigned to a given day.

Generally, graduate students make a daily action plan 1 week at a time to meet their weekly milestones. For example, imagine that we have a student who has an upcoming weekly milestone goal on his timeline to read relevant literature on social cognition and behavior change. That goal can be broken into a list of specific articles he needs to read. Then he can assign the tasks of reading each article to a specific day during the week. Exhibit 5.1 shows what his action plan for that particular milestone might look like.

In this action plan, only one milestone goal is broken down across the week. Usually, you will have multiple milestones you are striving to meet in a given week and have more actions planned each day. Exhibit 5.1 is simply an illustration of what breaking down a particular milestone into smaller tasks might look like.

Benefits of Action Plans

Overall, creating daily action plans on the basis of upcoming weekly milestones has four main benefits. First, creating a daily action plan helps you determine the specific tasks involved in achieving that milestone and provides a roadmap for each day. Thus, when you wake up in the morning you do not waste needless energy figuring out "where I'm going with my dissertation today." You can just look at your daily action plan and use that energy and time to actually achieve something.

A second benefit of creating action plans is that they can help you make better use of your time, especially when you only have small

---

EXHIBIT 5.1

Sample Action Plan

Milestone Goal = Read literature on social cognition and behavior change.

Action Plan

Monday
Read Ajzen, I. (2002) article on perceived behavioral control, self-efficacy, locus of control, and the theory of planned behavior.
Tuesday
Research job—no reading.
Wednesday
Read Bandura, A. (2001) article on social cognitive theory.
Thursday
Read Perry, C., Baranowski, T., & Parcel, G. (2002) article on social learning theory.
Friday
Read Prochaska, J. et al. (2003) article on how people change re: addictive behaviors.
Saturday
Read Armitage, C. J., & Conner, M. (2000) article on social cognition models and health.
Sunday
Day off from dissertation work.

windows of available work time. If you are like most graduate students, you often feel like you need several hours to make any meaningful progress on your dissertation. Yet in reality, your busy life does not always permit such windows of time. When you have clearly specified tasks, such as reading a journal article or running a particular statistical analysis, you can more readily dive in and get right to work. An action plan will also help you make better use of longer periods of available time, as accomplishing one small task after another can build a sense of momentum and motivate you to keep working. Daily success can cumulatively build your confidence and help you believe that finishing your dissertation is, in fact, possible.

A third benefit is that action plans help students feel a tangible sense of accomplishment on a regular basis. Students often tell me that no matter what dissertation tasks they complete, they rarely feel a sense of accomplishment because they are keenly aware of the long road ahead to the finish line and because there are few if any external rewards for completing tasks along the way. When you work without a plan and thus without a sense of where your dissertation activity begins and ends on a given day, it is easy to feel unsatisfied with whatever work you manage to accomplish. In addition, when you focus on how much you need to do in an overall sense, it is easy to feel unmotivated and un-inspired to do any dissertation work at all. In contrast, when you have a plan of specific, tangible work that you can accomplish for the day and you actually complete that work, you are more apt to feel satisfied and inspired to work the next day.

A fourth benefit is that action plans can be generalized and used as a way to manage all academic and nonacademic responsibilities and goals in your life, such as applying for a job, writing articles for publication, exercise, social events, religious or spiritual activities, and rest and relaxation. If you are like most graduate students, you may struggle to manage the multiple roles and responsibilities in your life. For example, many of my clients work full or part-time, are raising children, or are seeking to publish other research studies while they also work on their dissertations. Some students are caring for aging parents, managing a chronic illness, or in the process of applying for jobs. These activities directly compete with the dissertation and can make it difficult to make consistent progress. Creating weekly action plans can be a useful way to manage all of your roles and responsibilities. You can plan when you will work on specific dissertation tasks and when you will engage in non-dissertation-related activities at the outset of the week. So if, for example, you have a paper you are writing for publication, you can break it down into smaller tasks and put those tasks directly into the action plan. If you have certain exercise goals, you can incorporate them into your action plan.

Multiple Ways to Create Daily Action Plans

There is more than one way to make an action plan. In this chapter, I provide a variety of sample action plans so you can get a sense of what they look like and how you can create your own. I also include some general guidelines that my clients have found helpful in creating their own plans. Although there are no set rules for how you "should" create an action plan, these guidelines will help you become accustomed to making such plans.

GUIDELINE 1: MAKE ACTIONS SMALL AND SPECIFIC

An action is defined as a specific task you can complete in a relatively short time frame. I encourage students to aim to break down their milestone goals into tasks they can complete in 2 hours or less. I recognize that it is not always possible to know how long a task will take or to break your work down into such small intervals of time. The main aim, however, is to break down milestones into small enough chunks that the actions you need to take seem reasonable and less overwhelming to accomplish. Examples of common dissertation actions are reading a specific journal article or a book chapter, outlining or writing a rough first draft of a small subsection of a chapter, conducting one or two specific analyses, conducting an interview with a study participant, or making revisions to a drafted section of your dissertation. I recommend that you be as specific as possible when you create your action plan each week. Try to break down your milestones into a list of precise tasks that have a clear beginning and end that are close together such as "read pages 1 to 30 of Bandura's book" versus "read Bandura's book." The former task is more specific and realistic to accomplish than the latter task of reading an entire book in a day. There are times when a milestone goal on your timeline will already be a small enough task that you do not need to break it down further. For example, you may have a milestone that instructs you to set up a meeting with your chairperson or go to the library to obtain a book. Milestones such as these only need to be assigned to a day of the week in your action plan when you aim to complete them.

If you tend to procrastinate or feel anxious or overwhelmed by your dissertation work, I recommend that you make your actions very small. It is okay, for example, to plan to read only a few pages of an article, write a rough draft of a paragraph on a particular topic, or enter data for a small number of participants. Knowing that a task will only take a little bit of effort can make it much easier to believe you can complete the task and get to work even if you do not feel motivated.

GUIDELINE 2: CONNECT YOUR GOALS TO SPECIFIC DAYS OF THE WEEK

In addition to breaking down milestone goals from your timeline into specific actions, it is important to connect those actions to specific days of the week so that you know when you need to complete each action. If you merely have a list of actions you need to complete but do not have a plan of when to do each task, it is easy to put them off until later in the week. You then risk being unable to complete the larger milestones goals due for the week on your timeline. If you determine when you will really be able to complete each action on your list, then you will be more likely to actually complete those tasks. Also, you may benefit from specifying the time of day you plan to complete certain tasks and the particular place you will work (e.g., home, library, office, coffee shop). Purposively plan to work at times of day and in environments that are conducive to your own productivity.

You may decide that you can do more on a given day than you have planned and feel justifiably proud that you have not only met your goal but exceeded it. However, if you find yourself exceeding your daily goals on a consistent basis, you may be underestimating how much work you can accomplish daily and need to modify your plan accordingly. If you are never able to complete your daily goals even when you are working consistently, then you likely need to adjust in the other direction.

GUIDELINE 3: AIM TO MAKE A REALISTIC ACTION PLAN

It is very important to make action plans that are realistic. Planning to complete unrealistic amounts of work makes it unlikely you will meet your goals for the day. For example, if you work all day at a research job on Tuesdays and Thursdays, planning to come home in the evening and do hours of dissertation work on those days is likely unrealistic. Having an unrealistic plan that you cannot successfully complete will only make you feel bad about yourself and your ability to finish your dissertation in the long run and make you more likely to procrastinate the next day. You become discouraged about your ability to follow through on a plan. But the problem is not with your ability. The problem is that the plan is like a written setup for failure. Similar to my advice for creating your timeline, I encourage you to trust your instincts. If your gut instinct is that what you are planning to do in a day is unrealistic, then I advise you to rethink your plan and aim to be more realistic. Do your best to avoid using your action plan as an anxiety management tool. Writing down an unrealistic and long list of dissertation actions for each day may help you feel some immediate anxiety relief in terms of anxiety about finishing your dissertation, but it will not help you actually achieve your goals in the long run.

After many months, even years, of making unrealistic to-do lists, you may feel that you have no real gauge for what is realistic. Give yourself a few weeks or as long as you need to use the action plan structure to develop better instincts about what is realistic to accomplish in a given day. In the beginning, you may need to revise your plan a good deal, but if you are consistent about creating and revising your action plans you will develop a better sense of what is realistic over time. If being realistic is something that is a struggle for you, then I encourage you to make your plan with the assistance of another person who can help you be more honest about what you can accomplish on a day-to-day basis.

GUIDELINE 4: MAINTAIN YOUR ACTION PLANS IN AN ELECTRONIC FORMAT

Similar to my suggestion for making timelines, I encourage you to maintain your weekly action plans on your computer. Graduate students tend to ignore action plans when they are handwritten. Also, it is much easier to modify an action plan if it is on your computer. You can maintain two separate files—one for your dissertation timeline and one for your weekly action plan, or you can combine the two documents, inserting your weekly action plan below the timeline milestones the actions are designed to meet. Once you complete your upcoming milestones due at the end of the current week, then you can make a new action plan for the following week. You can make an action plan for more than 1 week at a time if you would find that helpful, but many find it easier to focus on 1 week at a time. Finally, when you keep your action plan in an electronic form you can easily e-mail it to those who are holding you accountable for your goals.

Examples of Action Plans

I have included four examples of action plans for you to review. Each student approached the creation of his or her action plan a little differently, depending on his or her dissertation goals and any other non-dissertation-related responsibilities. They all found a way to break down their larger milestone goals from their timelines into smaller, more specific actions. I hope these sample action plans will help you think about how you want to create your own action plans.

A STANDARD ACTION PLAN

In chapter 4, we reviewed a dissertation proposal timeline for a student named Samantha. She was writing her dissertation proposal and applying to clinical internship sites during the same period. By August 21, Samantha had three main milestone goals on her timeline that she wanted to accomplish: (a) write one section of her literature review on parental control and depression among adolescents, (b) write and mail letters requesting internship applications to 30 internship sites (a non-dissertation-related but significant milestone in her life), and (c) attend the American Psychological Association annual meeting that was being held in the city where she lived. She also planned when she would work at a university hospital and attend yoga classes. Samantha's plan is typical of how most of my clients create their plan, noting primarily dissertation actions and perhaps a few other important tasks or activities. Samantha found this level of detail in her action plan to be ideal for her (see Exhibit 5.2). You may require more or less detail in your plan. Samantha chose to put what she believed were key non-dissertation activities in italics. Also, Samantha's last action on the list—"Create a new action plan for the week of August 22 to August 28"—reminds her to make a new action plan for the week following this plan.

When reviewing Samantha's action plan, you will notice that she broke down the larger goal of writing a draft of the parental control and depression section of her literature review into a list of specific articles she needed to read and summarize. Also, she planned time to write up this section on Wednesday on the basis of the articles she had read up to that point. On Saturday, she planned to incorporate the articles she read Thursday and Friday about parental control and depression into what she had written on Wednesday. Then Samantha instructed herself to read the section, identify any missing points, review the literature to address any such points, and revise the drafted section. By breaking down the larger goal of writing the parental control and depression section of her literature review and assigning the actions to specific days, Samantha has done an excellent job of planning how she can meet this goal. Her action plan reads like an instructive to-do list that is realistic to accomplish on a daily basis. Each day Samantha wakes up to a clear, precise course of action she needs to take that, if completed, will result in her meeting her larger goal of writing a small section of her literature review and feeling successful at the end of the day.

THE DETAILED SCHEDULE ACTION PLAN

A sociology doctoral student named Beth created the next action plan. Beth's dissertation was a qualitative study examining women's experiences of sexual harassment in the workplace. In addition to being a doctoral student, Beth was working full time. At the time she wrote this action plan, she was in the midst of interviewing study participants and reading relevant sources to develop her literature review and better

EXHIBIT 5.2

Samantha's Action Plan

Samantha's Milestone Goals Due by August 21
1. *Written literature review section on parental control and depression.*
2. *Internship letters requesting applications written and mailed (15 sites).*
3. *Attend American Psychological Association Conference.*

Samantha's Action Plan to Meet Her August 21 Milestones

Monday August 15
- *Yoga at 10 a.m.*
- *Write generic letter requesting applications from internship sites.*
- Read and write summary of Petit, Laird, Dodge, Bates, et al. (2001).
- Read and write summary of Garber, Robinson, & Valentine (1997).
- Read and write summary of Barber, Olsen, & Shagle (1994).

Tuesday August 16
- *Work at university hospital from 8 a.m. to 6 p.m.*
- Read and write summary of Conger, Conger, & Scaramella (1997).
- Read and write summary of Baron & MacGillivray (1989).

Wednesday August 17
- *Attend APAGS internship workshop at APA conference from 9 a.m. to noon.*
- Write *rough* draft of parental control and depression section based on articles read to date.
- *Address envelopes for internship letters.*

Thursday August 18
- Read and write summary of Forehand & Nousiainen (1993).
- Read and write summary of Cole, Tram, Martin, et al. (2002).
- Read and write summary of Formosa, Gonzales, & Aiken (2000).
- Read and write summary of Herman, Dornbusch, Herron, & Herting (1997).
- *Yoga at 4 p.m.*

Friday August 19
- *Attend APA conference from 9 a.m. to noon.*
- Read and write summary of Barber (1996).
- Read and write summary of Mason, Cauce, Gonzales, & Hiraga (1996).
- *Customize internship letters for 10 sites.*

Saturday August 20
- Integrate literature read Thursday and Friday into parental control and depression section written on Wednesday to complete a rough draft of the entire section.
- Make a list of any points that might still be missing.
- Conduct search for any points that need additional literature.
- *Customize internship letters for 5 sites.*
- *Yoga at 4 p.m.*

Sunday August 21
- *Attend APA conference from 9 a.m. to noon.*
- Complete draft of parental control and depression section including any updates from list of points that are missing.
- Edit and revise parental control and depression section (print and edit at least twice).
- *Put all internship letters in envelopes, stamp, and have ready to mail on Monday.*
- Create a new action plan for the week of August 22 to August 28.

understand what she was learning from study participants. Beth had a demanding schedule, and she used the action plan structure to carefully manage her life so that she could realistically make consistent progress on her dissertation while working full time. Her action plan shown here is from the week of July 11 to July 17. Beth's four milestone goals due on July 17 (as planned in her timeline) were to (a) interview 2 study participants, (b) schedule two interviews for the following week, (c) transcribe one half of an interview, and (d) read select chapters in a book about sexual harassment litigation in the workplace.

Beth created a detailed schedule (Exhibit 5.3) of how her weekdays would flow from the time she woke up in the morning through the end of her day. Her plan detailed when she would complete dissertation tasks, work at her job, commute, eat, exercise, socialize, and even take a shower. Beth found it easier to stick to her plan when it had this level of detail. As I was the main person in Beth's life holding her accountable for meeting her dissertation work goals, she found it helpful to e-mail me with an update on her progress every few days. So you will notice a few times during the week that she plans to "e-mail update to Alison." Please note that Beth was going on vacation the week following the time frame of this plan. Thus, she planned to do a lot of dissertation work in the evenings after work because she would be unavailable the next week. I dissuade you from thinking you need to work at the same pace. You may want or choose to work more or less depending on you life's circumstances.

In general, I recommend that you do not plan to do dissertation work when you are on vacation. Unless you are under a tight deadline when you cannot leave your dissertation behind, I think it is best to make a vacation a true vacation. When students plan to do work on a vacation, they bring all kinds of books, articles, and research materials with them only to let them sit in their suitcase the entire trip. The mere presence of all of those dissertation materials makes them feel guilty, and it is hard to fully enjoy the vacation. A better alternative is to have an action plan ready for the day you return so that you can take advantage of the energy and perspective you have gained from having a real break from your daily routine.

Action Plan Templates

Another way to make and maintain a weekly action plan is to create an action plan template for the week, which is basically a written schedule of your general weekly routine. For example, a doctoral student, Jennifer, created the following template to help her have greater control over her

EXHIBIT 5.3

Beth's Detailed Action Plan

Beth's Milestones Due by July 17
1. Conduct two interviews (21 and 22) with study participants.
2. Schedule at least two interviews for next week.
3. Transcribe half of Interview 21.
4. Read chapters 1, 2, and 4 of litigation book.

Beth's Action Plan to Meet Her July 17 Goals

Monday July 11
6:00–7:00 a.m. Shower and get ready for work.
7:00–8:00 a.m. Get materials ready for Interviews 21 and 22.
8:00–9:00 a.m. Breakfast and commute to work.
9:00 a.m.–4:00 p.m. Work—leave by 4 p.m. to get to interview on time.
Noon. Talk to Alison; adjust action plan and timeline as needed.
5:00 p.m. Interview Study Participant 21.
8:00–10:00 p.m. Dinner and record observations and insights from Interview 21.

Tuesday July 12
6:00–8:00 a.m. Exercise and shower.
8:00–9:00 a.m. Breakfast and commute to work.
9:00 a.m.–5:00 p.m. Work.
5:00 p.m. Meet Sarah for coffee.
7:00–7:30 p.m. Call 2 potential study participants to schedule for week after vacation.
7:30 p.m.–10:00 p.m. Dinner and read chapter 1 of litigation book.
E-mail update to Alison.

Wednesday July 13
6:00–8:00 a.m. Exercise and shower.
8:00–9:00 a.m. Breakfast and commute to work (take materials for Interview 22).
9:00 a.m.–4:00 p.m. At work—leave by 4 p.m. to get to interview on time.
5:00 p.m. Interview Study Participant 22.
8:00–10:00 p.m. Dinner and record observations, thoughts, insights from Interview 22.

Thursday July 14
6:00–8:00 a.m. Exercise and shower.
8:00–9:00 a.m. Breakfast and commute to work.
9:00 a.m.–5:00 p.m. Work.
7:30–10:00 p.m. Dinner and read chapter 2 of litigation book.
E-mail update to Alison.

Friday July 15
6:00–8:00 a.m. Exercise and shower.
8:00–9:00 a.m. Breakfast and commute to work.
9:00 a.m.–5:00 p.m. Work; run any last minute errands for next week's trip at lunchtime.
6:00 p.m. Dinner and movies (meet Jim at Francesca's restaurant).

Saturday July 16
Morning: Read chapter 4 of litigation book.
Afternoon: Transcribe ¼ of Interview 21.
Evening: Anne's party.

Sunday July 17
Morning: Pack for trip next week.
Afternoon: Transcribe ¼ of Interview 21.
Evening: Make a new action plan for week after I return from vacation—send it to Alison.
Clean off desk and have action plan ready for week of July 26.

week and all of her responsibilities. Jennifer had 4 children age 9 and younger and a busy household. She created this detailed template (Exhibit 5.4) as a way to give herself a routine and determine when she would typically fulfill her academic and nonacademic goals and responsibilities. She planned specific zones of time Monday through Thursday each week to work on her dissertation. You will notice those time zones in bold in the following plan.

Each week, Jennifer used this template to create a new action plan in which she specified what dissertation tasks she would complete in each of the "dissertation zones" on Monday through Thursday. The actions planned in the dissertation zones were based on her milestones for the given week. For the sake of brevity, I am only including Monday and Tuesday in this text. Her template for Wednesday and Thursday was quite similar. What you cannot see here in the print of this book is that Jennifer chose to color code her action plan so that each area of her life was represented by a different color. For example, her dissertation time was in red, family activities were in blue, personal time

EXHIBIT 5.4

Jennifer's Action Plan Template

Monday
  5:30–6:30 a.m. Cardio workout.
  6:30–7:30 a.m. Get kids ready for school (Husband takes kids to school).
  7:30–8:30 a.m. Walk dog.
  8:30–9:00 a.m. Shower and get dressed.
  9:00 a.m.–2:30 p.m. Dissertation Zone (work at home)
  2:30–3:00 p.m. Walk dog.
  3:00–4:00 p.m. Housecleaning.
  4:00–5:30 p.m. Prepare dinner with 2 children.
  4:00–5:30 p.m. Kids do homework and practice instruments.
  5:30–6:00 p.m. Dinner and menu planning with family.
  6:00–7:30 p.m. Family playtime, walk, reading, prep for bed.
  8:00–10:00 p.m. Me time.
Tuesday
  5:30–6:00 a.m. Shower and get dressed.
  6:00–6:30 a.m. Walk dog.
  6:30–7:30 a.m. Get kids ready for school.
  7:30–8:30 a.m. Take husband to work and kids to school.
  8:30 a.m.–1:30 p.m. Dissertation Zone (work at husband's office).
  1:30–3:30 p.m. Grocery shop and errands.
  3:30–4:30 p.m. Pick up kids and husband.
  4:30–5:30 p.m. Prepare dinner with 2 children.
  5:30–6:00 p.m. Dinner.
  6:00–7:30 p.m. Family playtime, walk, reading, prep for bed.
  8:00–10:00 p.m. Me time.

was in green, and household responsibilities were in purple. You may find it helpful to use different colors in your own action plan. Exhibit 5.5 shows how Jennifer modified the template for 2 actual planned days (Monday and Tuesday) of a particular week. For the 2 days selected here, you can see that she listed the specific dissertation actions she plans to complete in the dissertation time zones.

From week to week, Jennifer's basic schedule did vary from the template, and she adjusted the action plan accordingly. For example, one week Jennifer was unable to work on a Wednesday after coming down with a bad cold. Thus she moved Wednesday's work to Thursday and was able to schedule an extra 3 hours of work on the weekend to complete the actions originally planned for Thursday. The point of a template is to give you a general routine, not a rigid plan your must adhere to at all times. If you choose to make an action plan template, be flexible in adjusting it from week to week depending on what is happening in your life while striving to protect time for your dissertation as much as possible.

EXHIBIT 5.5

Jennifer's Dissertation Zone Action Plans

Monday November 3
9:00–2:30 Dissertation Zone
Run step-wise regression to identify predictors for model.
Prep for testing model by cleaning other scales and predictors found through regression.
Conduct analysis to describe study sample including the following:
1. Child's grade level
2. Child's gender
3. Relationship to child
4. Other children at Rosemont (grade and #)
5. How long parent at Rosemont
6. Education level
7. Race
8. GED at school
9. Country
10. Time in US
11. Employment
12. Any employment
13. Hours worked
14. Spanish vs. English

Tuesday November 4
8:30–1:30 Dissertation Zone (at husband's office)
Look into books Mark recommended for structural equation modeling (order at least one).
Fill out IRB renewal form.
Find out when I can take ethics training on the Web.
Complete any remaining work from the earlier part of the week.

Short-Term and Vague Action Plans

Sometimes you may be in a position where making an action plan for an entire week will not be possible. For example, you may have a milestone goal of drafting a section of a chapter but have no outline or clear sense of what you need to write. Thus, the specific steps to meet that goal are not evident. You may need to spend the first few days of the week thinking, outlining, and free writing (see chap. 6, this volume, section on beginner's drafts) to develop a sense of what you will write and what actions you will need to take to meet your goals. In a situation such as this, make your action plan for as many days as it is clear what you need to do. Plan the specific reading, free writing, outlining, analyses, or other work you need to do to clarify your course of action. Once you have completed that work and can more clearly see what steps you need to take next, you can make your plan for the rest of the week.

The action plan shown in Exhibit 5.6 is an example of what a short-term plan might look like. In this situation, the student wants to update his literature review for his final dissertation. He has an existing literature review that he wrote for his proposal, but it needed to be further developed for his final dissertation and updated with any new research published since the time of his proposal. At the outset of the week, this student was not sure what sections of his literature review would need updating until he read his previous writing and conducted a literature search. Thus, he planned to do 2 days of work (reading and searching databases of published articles) to identify a clear course of action. On Tuesday, he noted that he would need to revise his plan for Wednesday through Sunday once he had a better sense of direction.

EXHIBIT 5.6

Short-Term Action Plan

Monday April 2
 Reread literature review from dissertation proposal.
 Make a list of areas that need further development or updating.
Tuesday April 3
 Conduct a literature search to identify articles to beef up proposal literature review.
 Download articles–go to library as needed.
 Revise plan for Wednesday through Sunday to determine when I will read articles and update various parts of the literature review (some of this reading and updating is likely to continue into next week's action plan).
Wednesday April 4 to Sunday April 8
 To be determined.

If you can only make a short-term plan, just keep planning as you get more information and a clearer sense of what you need to do. What is important is to maintain your role of project manager and find some way to structure your work for at least the next day. What follows are some guidelines to improve your use of action plans.

Don't Make Action Plans Alone

Similar to my advice for making timelines, you may want to seek outside help to create your weekly action plans, especially when you are new to the practice. It is often hard to realistically assess what you can accomplish in a given day. It is probably easiest to have the same person who helps you make your timeline help you make your action plans. Such assistance can help you regain the ability to make more accurate estimates of what you really can do on a day-to-day basis.

Align Your Action Plans With Your Values

Each action on your plan represents a value that is important to you. Yet it is easy to remain unaware of the connection between your daily goals and the larger values you care about. For example, when you are committed to reading research articles, writing a draft of a subsection, or running a specific statistical analysis, what larger values do those goals represent? Do they serve as a way for you to demonstrate your commitment to intellectual contribution, learning, achievement, integrity, and so on? Although it may not be immediately apparent, if you stop and think about how completing a particular goal is connected to your larger vision for your life, you will be able to see the connection between your goals and values.

Completing your dissertation still represents important values for you even if you feel lost right now or uncertain whether you want to work in your field of study post-graduate school. I do not believe you would be reading this book if you did not at least desire to demonstrate the value of integrity by keeping your promise to yourself (and perhaps your family) that you would finish. I encourage you to reflect on your values regularly as you work your way through your action plan. In this way, you can better align your behavior with the directions in life that are most important to you.

Revising Action Plans

No matter how carefully you make an action plan for a given week, you will not always be able to follow it. Just as timelines need frequent revision, so do action plans. Things happen. You may get sick, procrastinate, or underestimate how long a given task will take. Sometimes the work you plan takes a different direction, requires you to access additional information, or is more difficult than anticipated. Action plans are your best guess at the outset of the week as to what you can realistically do on a day-to-day basis. No matter how carefully you plan, reality will inevitably collide with your best intentions. I know that this is not your preference. I understand that you probably wish you could make a plan and simply stick to it. This does happen from time to time, but the reality is that you are human, imperfect, and that your plans will need revision. Keeping a flexible attitude about your work plans will help you better handle that reality. Be careful not to escalate your preference to stick to your plan as it is written into a demand that you absolutely must follow it. When students make unrealistic demands about following their action plans and are consequently unable to do the work as it is planned, I notice they end up feeling bad, inadequate, and even worthless.

Do your best each week to remain active in your role as project manager throughout the week. You will benefit from actively monitoring and managing your plan. Check in with your plan at the end of each day. Are you on track? Are you behind? Some weeks you complete your actions faster than they are planned and other weeks you get stuck on the very first action. Whatever happens, I highly recommend that you take the time to revise your plan when needed. If you get behind on your action plan, resist the temptation to simply dump all of the work you did not accomplish from the previous few days into the later days of the week. There may be occasions when moving work forward without adjusting the overall plan will work, but usually it results in an unachievable plan. Try to make an honest assessment of whether there is some way to get caught up by the end of the week, such as omitting or delegating another task. If not, then you may need to revise your overall timeline because if you will not be able to complete your actions for the week, you will not be able to complete your timeline milestones for the week.

Many of my clients purposely put aside 1 day each week to catch up on work that may be incomplete from earlier in the week. Some extra time to complete actions that were not completed as planned can help you make up for the delays most students inevitably experience. Be careful, however, not to use your catch up day as a reason to procrastinate on tasks earlier in the week (e.g., I can skip Tuesday's work because I have a catch-up day on Friday). Catch-up days are best spent dealing with the curves life throws you, not throwing a curve to yourself.

My clients who make the most consistent progress over time are those who actively step into the role of project manager and modify their actions plans when modifications are needed. They are not perfect. They procrastinate, they get stuck, and they underestimate how long various tasks will take. But they also make a consistent effort to actively manage their action plans and timelines and recommit to making progress.

Being a Project Manager

Being a project manager who consistently creates and revises the dissertation timeline and action plans is fundamentally about managing your energy so it is directed toward your value-driven goals. You have only a finite amount of energy in a given day, week, or month to direct toward your dissertation. When you spend some of that energy carefully planning your work on a week-to-week and day-to-day basis, you actually free up a great deal of energy so that it is available and ready to harness in the direction of completing actual dissertation work.

The structured approach of creating timelines and action plans is an important way to motivate you to do one of the most important dissertation tasks: writing. But this approach is not always sufficient by itself. In chapter 6, you will learn a variety of strategies to be more motivated and productive when it comes to writing. Use of these strategies can improve your ability to complete the writing goals you articulate as part of your timeline and action plans.

Writing and Revising Your Dissertation | 6

B y now you know that I believe in using a structured approach to complete your dissertation. I have witnessed many students use this approach to become substantially more motivated and productive on their journey to earning a doctoral degree. Even with structure, however, there are times when you will feel confused, overwhelmed, and unmotivated. In particular, students tend to struggle most with the work of writing their dissertations.

Blocks to writing progress can be overcome in a variety of ways, as attested by my coaching clients who were stuck but have nonetheless finished their dissertations. Depending on their personalities, these clients were able to choose among the strategies that I discuss in this chapter and make consistent progress in writing, even when they have been at an impasse for some time.

As you read the strategies in this chapter, I suggest you put a sticky note on the ones that seem to fit your personality. However, before you decide against trying any particular strategy, be sure to read it through with an open mind. It may be that you are reacting negatively because the strategy is different from your usual approach. In these cases, something different may be just what you need.

The chapter is divided into eight sections. Each section contains one or more strategies to consider. The first section discusses the perils of perfectionism and behavioral ways to let go of this tendency. The second section describes attitudinal changes that can help you when you are feeling stuck but are not sure why. The third section focuses on blocks in your environment (e.g., distractions) and how to minimize them. The fourth strategy offers advice on making writing a priority. The fifth section describes strategies to deal with the block many students feel when they are trying to transition from home, class, work, or family into working on their dissertations. The sixth section describes ways to light your fire when you are simply feeling unmotivated. The seventh section describes specific strategies to revise your dissertation. The final section addresses the all-important interim personal rewards that you can give yourself to stay motivated from writing the first to the last word of your dissertation.

Before you read these sections, I want to mention an all-important way to keep from (literally) losing it while you are writing your dissertation: backing up your work. Backing up your writing is an important way to protect yourself from losing your hours of hard work. Even if you have never lost a hard drive, had a serious computer virus, or experienced some other serious computer mishap, you can lose electronic versions of your dissertation at any point. I have witnessed too many clients lose their work and need to spend long hours recreating previous writing or data sets. A simple backup strategy is to e-mail your work to an online account on a regular basis that exists independent of your computer. You can also back up to online backup services, external drives, or CDs. Whatever you do to back up, make sure you have a consistent and sound strategy for ensuring that your work is protected.

Overcoming Perfectionism

In this section I look at a common problem that students encounter at this phase of their graduate work: perfectionism and strategies to overcome it. First, I discuss overcoming perfectionism, using your computer as an analogy. Second, I discuss the very important strategy of writing beginner drafts. Finally, I explore a helpful rule to move you from paralysis to action when you start your writing day.

PERFECTIONISM AND YOUR DISSERTATION

Perfectionism is a common obstacle to productivity among doctoral students. As discussed in chapter 2, perfectionism is generally defined as maintaining standards that are unrealistically high and impossible to attain (Hewitt & Flett, 1991). Some students impose excessively high standards for their writing that are unrealistic and unattainable. For example, many students believe they should be able to write a first draft that is ready to be reviewed by their advisor without ever needing to rewrite and revise over time. Other students believe that their dissertation chairperson, committee members, or other academics hold extremely high standards for their work that must be met to avoid disapproval. In response to their own excessive standards or those they believe are being imposed by others, perfectionist students often struggle to maintain their motivation and productivity. The pressure of living up to unrealistic standards can actually diminish the eagerness and desire to work because the emphasis on performing well is so great.

When it comes to completing a dissertation, many students believe that if they are perfect and do not make any mistakes, then they can be in control and protect themselves from seeming or being flawed. If you pursue perfection, it is likely your way of ensuring that you avoid exposing your perceived inadequacies. The pursuit of perfection may also be a way for you to maintain a sense of control and quell the uncertainty and anxiety inherent in the dissertation process. Seeking perfection, however, is an elusive goal that only gives you the illusion of control. No matter how many beautifully crafted sentences you write or how well you analyze and interpret your findings or argue your central thesis, you will likely still be able to find flaws with your work (and so will others). In life, we cannot protect others from seeing that we are not perfect (and in real life people rarely expect you to be perfect), nor can we avoid seeing our own fallible nature. It is virtually impossible to write a dissertation that is above criticism. In fact, striving to research and write a perfect dissertation would likely require such great effort that other parts of your life (e.g., health, well-being, relationships) would suffer. Writing a "perfect" dissertation will not lead to redemption where all concerns and feelings of inadequacy are permanently banished from your life. You will just earn a PhD and believe that your next endeavor needs to be even more perfect.

It is important to keep in mind that faculty members will almost certainly suggest that you make some changes or encourage you to think about your work in different ways (especially when you are developing a dissertation proposal). Receiving feedback and being asked to modify your work is a normal part of the dissertation process. You would be better off expecting feedback rather than striving for perfection. Remember, you have the capacity to handle feedback, even if it feels like criticism when you receive it. Paradoxically, striving for perfection can be like sentencing yourself to always underperforming, to always being insufficient, and never being able to measure up to what are actually unrealistic and unreasonable expectations. Most perfectionists would not expect of others what they expect of themselves (although there are some perfectionists who have excessive standards for others). Yet if you are a perfectionist, you likely pursue this goal to the exclusion of reason and the advice of others.

When it comes to writing, perfectionism has a particularly potent and negative effect on students' ability to build momentum and write productively. If your aim is perfection (especially when writing a first draft), then you block your ability to let ideas flow and build momentum. Anne Lamott (1994) described perfectionism as "the voice of the oppressor, the enemy of the people. It will keep you cramped and insane your whole life, and it is the main obstacle between you and a shitty first draft" (p. 28). I have witnessed countless students struggle to write a first draft as they are stifled by the pursuit of perfection.

Here is an analogy to put the impact of perfectionism on writing into perspective. Think about your experiences working with computers. You have probably had the experience of using a computer when you had a large number of software programs open simultaneously. Perhaps the computer started running slowly, you had to reboot the system because it was freezing up, or it crashed and shut down entirely. Something similar happens to your ability to build and sustain momentum when you write. Writing a dissertation is by definition an involved, complex task. If we stick with the computer program analogy, we could describe writing a dissertation as involving many types of "writing programs." Often, when you run too many writing programs, you start writing in a slow and halting manner, you freeze up and shut down, moving into procrastination and avoidance mode. Some examples of common writing programs you may be using when you write follow:

- Determine what I want to say about specific existing research or particular theories.
- Clearly explain existing theories, concepts, and existing research findings.
- Synthesize my own ideas with previous research.
- Cite my references and make sure I do not plagiarize.
- Write well-formed, intelligent-sounding sentences.
- Use correct spelling and grammar.
- Create good transition between sentences, paragraphs, and chapter sections.
- Clearly articulate the purpose of my study.
- Make sure my argument is strong.
- Make sure my writing is well organized.

There are other more advanced programs graduate students "run," such as,

- What will my advisor or committee think of my work?
- Will I pass my dissertation defense?
- Will I be able to publish my dissertation?
- Will my dissertation be good enough to get an academic job?

Imagine sitting down to write with many or all of these writing programs running simultaneously. That is a lot of strain on your system. You may come to dread writing, putting it off as long as possible or struggle to develop and maintain momentum. Perfectionists usually try to write with all or far too many writing programs open at once. They often hope that if they can just write the first draft perfectly, they will not have to go back and edit anything or be seen as incompetent or inadequate. Yet writing, especially academic writing, is challenging. You will need to rewrite and revise your work over time. Striving for perfection, especially in the early stages of writing, is a surefire way to "shut down your system."

Any time writing is not going well, examine the expectations you have of yourself. Are you making excessive demands? Are you expecting too much for a first draft? Do you believe that you should be able to write prolifically, sailing through paragraphs without stopping? Do you believe that other people write with ease and that only incompetent or inadequate people struggle? Are you using a particular writing program at the wrong time in the writing process, such as worrying about transitions and grammar or what your committee will think of your work when you write your first draft?

The guideline that I give most students is to begin writing a first draft with only a few writing programs open at a time. For example, if you are writing a literature review, you may only want to open the "determine what I want to say about specific existing research or particular theories" and "clearly explain existing theories, concepts, and existing research findings" programs. Of course, you will want to use the "make sure I don't plagiarize" program. It can also be a good idea to cite your references as you write, as it can be a lot of work to go back and do this task later. Resist the temptation to use the "what will my advisor think" program at this point. Go back after the basic content is down and improve the draft using various writing programs as needed. Get feedback from others when you are stuck (this is a very important and often neglected writing program).

Letting go of perfectionism ultimately means that you need to find a way to trust that your writing and your dissertation are evolving over time. Your work on any given day may not seem satisfactory, but if you hang in there, keep writing, revising, and integrating the input of others (e.g., your advisor and committee members), you will eventually have a product of sufficient quality to earn a doctoral degree. It may be a messier road than you might like, but a messier road may be a quicker and actually less painful road than a perfectly paved one.

BEGINNER'S DRAFTS: AN ANTIDOTE TO PERFECTIONISM

Among the best advice I ever received on being a more productive writer was to allow myself to write *beginner's drafts.* Virtually, every book on writing I have read covers the importance of being willing to write a beginner's draft; a rough-all-over-the-place messy draft that no one will see but you as a way to begin writing and get your writing juices flowing, ideas percolating, and actual words down on the page. What all of these authors know firsthand from their own writing experience and witnessing other writers write is how challenging and even painful writing the first draft can be. They also know that a major reason writers do not let themselves write beginner's drafts is because they believe other writers do not need to write them. Anne Lamott (1994) in her book *Bird by Bird* aptly describes the myths people often believe about successful authors and the contrast of what the writing experience is really like for them:

> People tend to look at successful writers . . . and think that they sit down every morning feeling like a million dollars, feeling great about who they are and how much talent they have . . . they take in a few deep breaths, push back their sleeves, roll their neck a few times to get all of the cricks out, and dive in, typing fully formed passages as fast as a court reporter. But this is just the fantasy of the uninitiated. I know some very great writers, writers you love who write beautifully and have made a great deal of money and not one of them sits down routinely feeling wildly enthusiastic and confident. . . . Very few writers really know what they are doing until they've done it . . . They do not type a few stiff warm up sentences and then find themselves bounding along like huskies on the snow. . . . We all often feel like we are pulling teeth, even for those writers whose prose ends up being the most natural and fluid. . . . For me and most of the other writers I know, writing is not rapturous. In fact the only way I can get anything written at all is to write really, really shitty first drafts. (pp. 21–22)

It is common for graduate students to make the same erroneous comparison with academics and researchers who have published books and articles in their research area. They look at published research and forget that they are reading the final, revised, and edited version. The published work has usually been through peer review or careful developmental editing by a publisher. There were certainly previous and much rougher drafts with errors, holes in logic, omissions, and big messes. What you read in print is the polished end product. If you keep comparing your efforts with this product, you are bound to feel inadequate.

Certainly, there are academics who are very prolific writers who are able to write a literature review in a weekend or churn out pages of beautiful prose overnight. But there is one significant difference between those academics and you: experience. They have simply engaged in more academic writing than you and become proficient at it over time. You, however, are unlikely to have that kind of experience at this juncture in your life. This fact may not be your preference, but I encourage you to avoid demanding that you must be able to write at the same level as more experienced academics. If you are committed to writing well, you will improve with continued practice and experience but that takes time. Bolker (1998) encouraged students to think of beginner's drafts as the opportunity to make a mess so you have something to clean up, improve over time, and eventually turn your work into a piece of writing you feel good about.

Beginner's drafts are about letting yourself write with abandon, letting go of concerns about spelling, grammar, word choice, sentence structure, meaning, style, organization, or your argument. The main goal of writing at this stage is to just keep writing and get something down on paper (Bolker, 1998). Stephen King (2002), in his book *On Writing: A Memoir of the Craft,* described the first draft as the draft you write with the "office door closed." It is the draft you write without consideration of your audience and only after you have something drafted, is it appropriate to "crack the door open" and begin to consider your audience as you revise and improve your draft. Graduate students often write their first draft as if their advisor or committee is sitting there in the room reading what they are writing. They would do well to "close the office door" when they write early drafts and let go of concerns about what their advisor or committee would think of their work at this stage. Beginner's drafts are about lowering your standards temporarily so you can actually complete some writing. You can have high standards for your writing eventually, but you are not likely to be a prolific dissertation writer if you have high standards from the start.

Two objective behaviors can help you make the shift to writing beginner's drafts. The first is picking a narrow, specific writing goal that is something you can reasonably accomplish in a day. A narrow writing goal can make it easier to let go of high standards for a first draft if you know you will be drafting just one small part of your dissertation. Second, plan time in your timeline or action plan to write beginner's drafts. Many of my clients actually plan to write "crappy," "shitty," "beginner," "high school level," or "rough, rough" drafts of specific subsections of their dissertation in their timeline or action plans. Then at some later date (even the next day), they plan time to revise the draft. Knowing that they have planned time to revise in the future helps them let go and just write a beginner's draft in the present. I know writing beginner's drafts may feel uncomfortable and awkward, but it is important if you want to become a more productive writer. Keep practicing letting go of excessive standards for your writing, and give yourself the gift of seeing how freeing it can be to write a beginner's draft and revise it later. You may find that writing this way becomes second nature and that consequently you get a lot more writing done.

THE 15-MINUTE RULE

The *15-minute rule* is one of my favorite strategies for helping students let go of high standards and just write. This strategy is also useful for helping you write when you have little motivation to do so. Bolker (1998) recommended that students begin by writing for an absolute minimum of 10 minutes every day and then expand to 15 minutes and then to longer periods. She suggested that students make a commitment that no matter what, they will absolutely write for 10 minutes a day. Bolker wrote, "Anyone can write for 10 minutes a day, particularly if one is free writing" (p. 41). I usually recommend that students work for a minimum of 15 minutes but the number is somewhat arbitrary, as long as it is enough time to help you get warmed up to working on your dissertation.

Many people find that committing to dissertation work for a relatively short amount of time, such as 15 minutes, makes it easier to make the transition to a meaningful writing session. Here is how it works. You commit to working on any relevant part of your dissertation for an absolute minimum of 15 minutes. I recommend setting a timer if possible. You set the timer and start working. If you are writing, then write with abandon, letting go of concerns about sentence structure, flow, spelling, or grammar. You just write your ideas as they come out of your head. If critical voices pop in your head, then write down what they have to say. If extraneous thoughts pop into your head, then write them down too with the aim of getting back to your dissertation and staying on task as much as possible. When the 15 minutes is over, you can stop and highlight what you want to keep and the rest you will ignore. Or you can keep going if you are so inspired. Often, my clients tell me that once the 15 minutes are over, they feel warmed up to writing and it is easier to continue. A short period of forced writing, in which you commit to writing no matter how much you do not feel like working, can often get you over the motivational hump and lead to a productive writing session. Sometimes, students need several planned 15-minute periods in a day to help them stay on course as motivation and energy for writing ebbs and flows throughout the day for most writers.

The 15-minute rule can be a great way to deal with the basic fact that warming up to writing a beginner's draft can be difficult. No matter how detailed your action plan and timeline are or how inspired you felt the night before, when you wake up in the morning you may feel like a thick fog of apathy rolled in during your sleep. The next thing you know, hours, even days go by and you have completed little or no meaningful work. Inspiration and motivation rarely come from inaction. Every day that you intend to work but do nothing puts you at risk of becoming disengaged from your dissertation and makes it that much harder to get started in your next work session. It is often the act of writing, making discoveries, articulating and connecting ideas, or analyzing data or sources that will inspire and motivate you.

Am I saying that you need to work first before you are motivated and inspired to write a beginner's draft? Yes. Sure, there are times when you are raring to go first thing in the morning. But if you wait for those days to just happen to you, your dissertation may take a long time to complete. I suggest that you commit to working a minimum of 15 minutes two to three times a day as a way to get your intellectual juices flowing and to motivate yourself when you are struggling to work consistently. Staying connected to your dissertation (even if all you do is read previous writing) is an important way to keep the fires of motivation and inspiration alive. Do your best to write or do other dissertation work for at least 15 minutes. When the 15 minutes are over, push yourself to go for 5, 10, or 15 minutes more. Stretch out the work for as long as you can. Then plan another 15-minute session later in the day and repeat your efforts to stretch the work session longer. If you consistently engage in the 15-minute rule, then you will likely be able to work for longer periods on a regular basis.

Overcoming a Negative Mind-Set Toward Writing

A negative mind-set toward writing your dissertation may have many sources, from innate personality styles to previous painful experiences. Whatever the source, you can do something about a mind-set that sabotages you in your daily writing efforts. In this section we look at two important strategies for overcoming a negative mind-set without attempting to change your overall personality or your history. First, I look at an often-ignored roadblock to progress: difficulty tolerating ambiguity and how you might improve your ability to do so. Second, I discuss how competing with others gets in your way and how you can make changes in this regard.

LEARN TO TOLERATE AMBIGUITY

I remember some very good advice I received from James G. Kelly, PhD, a faculty member who served on my dissertation committee. My dissertation required very involved qualitative analyses. In our conversations about my research, he consistently told me that one of the most important qualities I could develop as a doctoral student and as a researcher was the ability to tolerate ambiguity. He stressed that academic research and writing is filled with moments when the appropriate course of action is not evident, when more questions are apparent than answers. He emphasized that being able to tolerate the inherent ambiguity in academic research is crucial to success. Dr. Kelly encouraged me to be more tolerant of ambiguity in my own research so that I would not rush to premature conclusions about my interview data with homeless adults. He believed it was important to wade around not knowing the answers while delving deeper, asking more questions, and being thoughtful about what stories my data had to tell. Being tolerant of ambiguity during the writing process is also a key to success. Such tolerance will increase your willingness to write a beginner's draft and help you be more patient and less judgmental of yourself when writing does not come easily.

How do you develop more tolerance of ambiguity? A key strategy is to keep your expectations and standards, especially in the early stages of writing, in check. Personally, I actively remind myself that my writing in any given day may be of less quality or clarity than I would like. Sometimes writing comes easily and other times I am confused and struggle to organize my thoughts and articulate or express my ideas on paper. Even as I wrote this book, my original outline changed on a regular basis, and there were many times when the order and content of chapters seemed ambiguous. At many points, I had random notes and ideas written on scraps of paper, in various folders, and written directly into chapter drafts. Often, I did not know which notes and ideas were useful and relevant and which to disregard. When I am engaged in writing, I do my best to believe that I will eventually transform my chaotic, messy, all-over-the-place writing into something I would consider letting other people see. It is important to learn to trust that with time and consistent effort you will be able to make revisions, figure out how to write something that you could not express previously, and improve the quality of your work. Creating a well-crafted product does not usually happen in one or even several work sessions. You may end many work sessions feeling confused and uncertain. But if you can maintain tolerance for the ambiguity of the research process while being consistent in your efforts to read, analyze, clarify, revise, and improve your work, you will eventually have a product you can feel good about.

Cultivating a growth mind-set about intelligence (as discussed in chap. 3, this volume) is a second useful strategy to become more tolerant of ambiguity. People with a growth mind-set believe intelligence is malleable and can be increased through effort, guidance, and perseverance. People with a fixed mind-set believe intelligence is unchangeable (Dweck, 2006). I would surmise that people with a growth mind-set are more tolerant of the inherent ambiguity of conducting and writing a dissertation study. They are more apt to view intellectual challenges and difficulties with their dissertations as opportunities for learning and growth and as ways to increase their competence and mastery. They are more willing to struggle, ask for guidance, and try new approaches than are fixed mind-set theorists.

If you are someone who views intelligence as fixed, then tolerating ambiguity is likely to be more challenging for you. You may want answers to come easily, fearing that an intellectual struggle is a sign that you lack intelligence. If you lean toward having a fixed mind-set, I encourage you to use your dissertation and the difficulties you are bound to encounter as opportunities to practice being more tolerant of the discomfort associated with not knowing what to do. Be willing to write very rough drafts, try different data analysis approaches, seek guidance, explore ideas, struggle, and map out visual representations of your research questions, theoretical framework, or the argument you are trying to make (or find) over and over again. Be curious in the pursuit of finding your voice as a researcher. Keep exerting effort and try to see your dissertation as an intellectual adventure that can and will increase your intelligence if you let yourself struggle, ask for input, and pursue solutions without making premature evaluations of your intelligence. Struggle does not equal lack of intelligence. Struggle is inherent to the dissertation process and is the way to a good dissertation. So practice being more tolerant of ambiguity. You will be more productive as a result and perhaps be able to cultivate a growth mind-set as you see that persistence is an important avenue in working through intellectual struggles and becoming more competent.

REFUSE TO COMPETE

Many students think that competing and striving to outperform other people is an effective strategy to increase motivation and productivity. When you see others performing well, it can provide a healthy sense of peer pressure and incentive to get to work and make progress on your dissertation. Yet, all too often I see students competing in an unhealthy way where they are constantly comparing themselves with their peers, feeling good when they outperform their peers (or at least have comparable performance), and feeling bad when their peers outperform them. Competing with others can keep you stuck in the mode of proving yourself and believing that you must be more intelligent or competent than your peers. Competition reinforces the message that you need to be better than someone else. Why would you need to be better than someone else? Because deep down you feel inadequate or worry whether or not you have enough intelligence and competence to earn a PhD. Competition also reinforces the belief that intelligence is fixed and finite (Dweck, 2000). If you have a growth mind-set, you do not need to waste your time competing or comparing yourself because you know you can learn and grow more competent. So I encourage you to redirect your energy toward yourself, your values, your own goals, and what it will take for you to meet those goals. If you can focus more on yourself, you can regain the energy lost to worrying about other people's performance and how it compares with your own.

Dealing With Distraction

Distractions come in many forms. Some are environmental and best handled by directly intervening in your environment. Other distractions are self-imposed activities, especially those that are closely tied to your writing process, such as checking your e-mail. Still others occur when we lose focus on our values and values-driven goals. In this section we look at strategies to deal effectively with distractions in all forms so that you can concentrate on finishing your dissertation.

CREATING A CONDUCIVE ENVIRONMENT

A distracting, messy, and disorganized work environment can easily thwart your motivation to write and work on your dissertation. Look at your desk, file drawers, how your files are organized on your computer, and your work environment as a whole. Ask yourself whether what you see is conducive to productivity and being motivated. Often graduate students avoid cleaning up and organizing their work environment because they keep telling themselves that they do not have time to do so. It is very easy to keep pushing aside piles of paper and to ignore the mess in your office in pursuit of getting more dissertation work done. Yet the messy, disorganized environment may be interfering with your ability to get started, build momentum, and stay focused when you are writing.

The time it takes to organize your office, in particular, your dissertation materials, is well spent. I am not suggesting that you obsess about keeping a clean, organized work environment or let cleaning and organizing become a procrastination strategy. Rather, I recommend including weekly time on your action plan to clean and organize your office to prevent it from becoming cluttered and chaotic. If your work environment is currently in need of a lot of attention, it is worth dedicating the time to get it in order. You will benefit in future work sessions from having taken the time to get organized.

TAMING PHONE CALLS, E-MAIL, AND OTHER DISTRACTIONS

Your motivation to write, and your productivity, can also be thwarted by distractions in your physical environment. Something as simple as a phone call can distract you and make it difficult to regain your motivation and focus. During your next dissertation work session take note of the sights and sounds around you. What distracts you from staying focused and motivated? Do cell phone calls, people stopping by your office, text and instant messages, or e-mail alerts on your computer distract you and make it hard to stay on track? Think about what distracts you, and do your best to minimize those distractions. Also, consider that you may need to find new or different work environments that are more conducive to being productive.

If you are like the typical graduate student I meet, you may be a good candidate for an "e-mail intervention." Checking e-mail, responding to received e-mails, and composing new e-mails has become a habit (even maybe an addiction of sorts) for millions of Americans (Wright, 2006). I am quite certain that doctoral students rank among those who cannot seem to stop themselves from checking e-mail all day long. Many begin a given work session by opening up e-mail and usually delay dissertation work and then continuously interrupt work progress by checking it throughout the day.

In the spirit of candor, I am a reformed e-mail addict (who still relapses on occasion). I could start the charter chapter of E-mailers Anonymous. While I wrote the first four chapters of this book, I was completely hooked on my e-mail. Every time I sat down to write, I first opened my e-mail before launching into a planned writing session. The next thing I knew, 30 minutes or longer had passed and I had not written one word. Then, once I was writing, I would find myself compulsively checking my e-mail anytime I was tired, bored, uncertain, or even for no apparent reason. E-mail can seem like a good distraction and give you a little kick of adrenaline as you see what "urgent" messages await your response. The process of writing this book forced me to conduct an e-mail intervention on myself. You may be a good candidate for such an intervention (this may also apply to social networking sites, text messaging, instant messaging, surfing the Internet, or playing computer games). When I am writing, I keep my e-mail program closed. Otherwise I will hit the receive button in an involuntary fashion as if my right hand is possessed by an outside demonic force that demands, "Must check e-mail. Check it now."

When I am incapable of keeping my e-mail closed on a voluntary basis, I actually disable my wireless connection altogether by unplugging the wireless router in my husband's office and dropping the Ethernet cord on the floor behind a file cabinet where it is hard to reach (sad, I know, that I must resort to this strategy, but it works). I then use e-mail as a reward for writing. I allow myself to check it after a certain amount of work or at a certain time of day. Also, I do not work in coffee shops that have free wireless Internet access if I am bringing my computer. I regularly remind myself that it is highly unlikely that anyone is communicating a life or death matter to me over e-mail. I am sometimes desperate to check my e-mail and feel a little anxious wondering what is waiting in my inbox. But ultimately, I know that checking e-mail is a self-defeating distraction that limits my productivity and writing output. You may be thinking, "I can handle my e-mail. It isn't a problem for me. I can restrain myself when it is time to work." Maybe that is true, but I am guessing that you are just in denial.

Some of my clients list "disable their Internet connection" or "close down e-mail" as the first daily action on their action plan. I encourage you to think about your actual e-mail habits and then put some guidelines in writing in your weekly action plan that will help you structure when and for how long you will check your e-mail. This may seem unnecessary, but if you add up all the time you spend checking e-mail, you may be surprised at how much it takes. E-mail is something that is available all day long just waiting to interrupt you and your workflow. If you can put some firm limits on your use of e-mail, you will find it easier to be productive.

Ask yourself what bad habits you may have that are the equivalent of my e-mail addiction. Maybe you play hours of computer games, promising yourself that each new game is the last. You may surf the Internet mindlessly telling yourself that are going to get to work in 5 more minutes. Maybe you turn on the television for background noise and then find yourself sucked into three back-to-back episodes of *Law and Order*. You may also have some very sneaky bad habits. These are the kind of habits that at face value look like you are working on your dissertation. You are reading literature, making writing plans, working on your outline, or doing other dissertation-related tasks. Yet, what you are doing is not necessary and is peripheral to getting your butt in the chair and doing what you truly need to be doing. To be sure, reading literature, outlining, and so forth may be legitimate activities that are important precursors to writing. If you are honest with yourself, though, you know when they are valid activities or habitual ways of avoiding the real dissertation work you need to do.

Many of my clients resist changing their work habits because doing so is unpleasant and difficult. For example, when students initially attempt to develop better work habits, such as limiting e-mail use, writing beginner's drafts, or turning off the television, they feel uncomfortable and anxious. Thus, they revert to their old ways to relieve themselves from the tension and discomfort that the bad habits seem to mitigate. Changing bad habits does not necessarily feel good because you must face the negative feelings you would rather avoid. Yet if you know that your work habits interfere with your ability to be productive, what is your alternative? Is feeling tense or anxious as a result of limiting your access to e-mail or computer games worse than being angry with yourself for wasting time and failing to meet a deadline? Is being uncomfortable while you learn to lower your standards and write very rough drafts so much worse than feeling hopeless and demoralized by your lack of progress? I encourage you to be honest with yourself about your own unhelpful, self-defeating behavior and strive to change your work habits for the better.

Breaking bad work habits is fundamentally about making choices that will make you happier in the long run even if they feel uncomfortable in the short run (Wright, 2006). It takes focused, consistent effort to break bad habits and replace them with better, more productive behaviors. There will be setbacks and days where it does not seem that you are getting any reward from your efforts. Most people need continued practice engaging in new, positive behavior over several weeks for the behavior to become easier and more automatic. I do not promise that it will be easy, but developing better work habits can lead to more productive workdays and eventually to a finished dissertation.

Making Writing a Real Priority

The next strategy is learning to make your dissertation a priority. I realize that this seems obvious and that you may think that your dissertation is already a highly important priority in your life. Yet the actual behavior you engage in on a daily basis may tell another story. If I observed you in action over a week, would I see that you make your dissertation a priority? Often graduate students are thinking on a regular basis about their dissertations, but when it comes to actually doing the work, other activities seem to take precedence.

There is one category of activities that often upstages dissertation work. That category is tasks you perceive as being urgent. In life, there are tasks that are genuinely urgent, such as grading exams, completing course assignments, and paying your bills on time. Most dissertation activities are tasks that are important to complete, but they are not urgent. Rarely is there an immediate consequence if you do not complete a given dissertation task. Tasks that are important in life but not urgent often get pushed aside by people in favor of completing more seemingly urgent tasks, such as returning e-mail, doing laundry, or completing work for a research or teaching job. The urgent tasks seem to scream out, "Complete me first, I am a priority!" Certainly, it is important to complete urgent tasks. Your bills do need to get paid, you need to fulfill work and household responsibilities, and your e-mail requires attention. Yet it is important to balance completing urgent and non-urgent tasks if you want to make consistent progress on your dissertation. Think about your own behavior. Do you tend to maintain an "as soon as I . . ." attitude telling yourself that you will get to your dissertation tasks "as soon as" you complete something that seems more pressing? If you do not make your dissertation a priority, eventually it will no longer be a nonurgent project. Instead, you may be up against a department or university deadline with a great deal of pressure to finish on time. I doubt that you want to be in a situation in which you have to complete your dissertation under a constrained timeline.

I encourage you to use your action plan as a way to balance the need to complete both urgent and nonurgent tasks. As much as possible, plan specific time to work on your dissertation tasks. Completing these tasks will help you make consistent progress and build motivation and momentum to continue your work the next day. Finishing important, nonurgent tasks is what often gives people the greatest sense of satisfaction and fulfillment, as these tasks are an expression of their values-driven goals (Ditzler, 1994). There are times when you may need to devote more energy to urgent tasks, such as pressing family issues or teaching or work responsibilities. Once those more urgent tasks or issues are handled, aim to quickly rebalance the amount of time you dedicate to urgent and nonurgent tasks. In general, when you make your dissertation a priority, you will naturally complete the urgent tasks as well, because they are by definition urgent.

One way to make your dissertation more of a priority is to follow Bolker's (1998) suggestion to "write first." By "write first" she is suggesting that dissertation writers make writing their highest priority. This is wise advice. I encourage my clients to write first whenever possible. Write first before you check your e-mail, do your laundry, pay your bills, or do other academic work. A "write first" habit can be difficult to develop initially, but it is important nonetheless. Writing first is about setting up your life so that you can make writing a main focus and concern in life. If you choose an academic or research career after graduate school, developing this habit now will serve you well the rest of your life.

Something that helped me make writing this book a real priority was a news story I saw on television about a very serious fire that burned down hundreds of thousands of acres in San Diego, California. A significant reason that the fire was so devastating was a 100-year-old National Forest Service policy that directed firefighters to put out all fires immediately. At the time this policy was enacted, it was thought that putting out all fires was the right thing to do to protect the forest and surrounding communities. Yet this policy has a huge negative consequence. When fire is never allowed to burn in a forest, an enormous amount of fuel consisting of dead and dying trees and plants accumulates. If you mix in other conditions such as drought and high winds, the combination can lead to an explosive fire that is uncontrollable because of the large amount of fuel existing in the forest. Small, controlled fires are actually necessary for the health and greater good of a forest. If smaller fires had been allowed to burn in San Diego, there would have been less fuel and, likely, a less devastating fire.

On hearing this story, I recognized a similarity to what happens to students when they make urgent tasks a priority. In a sense, urgent tasks are like small fires burning in your life. When you keep putting out every fire and never let your e-mail, voice mail, work responsibilities, and so on "burn" for a while, the values-driven goals that are most important to you go up in flames. Even as I was writing this very section, I had phone calls to return, an inbox full of e-mail, and a long list of household chores to complete. But I reminded myself that I was going to temporarily let those "fires burn" for the greater good of meeting a significant goal: writing this book. Many of my clients have told me they find it freeing to remember that it is okay to do one thing at time and to focus their energy on their real priorities, even when many tasks are competing for their attention. On your quest to make your dissertation a real priority, remember that urgent tasks are burning, so you will not forget about them. Ultimately, though, it is necessary to let small fires burn if you want to make consistent progress on your dissertation.

Starting and Transitioning

Making writing a real priority and transitioning from work, home, family, and other obligations to doing the work of writing can be hard for anyone. I have already mentioned the 15-minute rule, and this should be part of your strategy if you find yourself backing away from your work before you even start. In this section, I discuss three other strategies that have helped my clients get going on a daily basis.

GET SET UP THE NIGHT BEFORE

A simple strategy to increase your motivation and make it easier to write is to find and organize the work materials you will need for the next day the night before your next planned session of work. Getting set up for the following day makes it easier to feel motivated when the next day arrives. Students often spend their energy and limited work time finding and organizing the research materials they need. It is easy to lose precious work time to such activities and feel unmotivated to begin working. I recommend ending your workday by making sure you have what you will need to work the next day. If you have a few articles to read, pull them out and, along with your action plan, put them on you desk or in the bag or backpack you will take with you the next day. Make sure you have easy access to any outlines, rough drafts, pertinent notes, and source material you will need. Taking the time to get organized ahead of time is a simple strategy you can use to kick-start your motivation and start writing.

PLAN SMALL ACTIONS TO START THE DAY

The strategy of planning small actions to start the day is the practice of carefully identifying an action that will not require too much motivation to start your workday. When you are creating your action plan it is a good idea to purposefully plan a writing goal that is small and specific to begin the day. Clearly identified, small writing goals can make it easier to warm up to working in a given work session. You may feel more motivated because it seems realistic that you can accomplish the task. You can clearly see the beginning and end of the task and can imagine yourself completing it. For example, if you wake up in the morning and your first action is to write a rough overview of one or two studies or revise a few pages you wrote the day before, it is easier to get started with less dread or hesitation. Of course, I know this is just a game of semantics, but I encourage you to try it. See for yourself if starting the day or work session with small, specific writing goals helps you feel more motivated and leads to greater overall productivity.

JUMP INTO THE POOL

After years of observing doctoral students, it is clear to me that there is one distinctive moment in time that creates the most problems for being motivated and productive. That moment is when a student needs to make the transition from not working or being engaged in their dissertation to doing actual, meaningful work. This is the moment when you transfer your energy and focus from checking your e-mail, watching television, organizing research materials, making an action plan, or engaging in any other activity to actually working on your dissertation. Students often struggle to make that transition, instead engaging in all kinds of alternate activities. Some students can only transition to doing meaningful work if a deadline looms or they feel stressed about how much work they need to do. I believe that it is important to be aware of this moment of transition and of how you can more quickly, easily, and successfully make that transition without deadlines or fear of negative consequences.

I like to think of making the transition to being actually engaged in dissertation work as similar to entering a pool that is below 80 degrees. (Okay, I am a bit of a wimp when it comes to my comfort level in a pool.) My parents have a beautiful pool in their backyard that always looks very inviting any time I walk out their back door. But my parents will not heat their pool. Despite my pleas, they stubbornly refuse to heat the pool, even for my children. They believe heating a pool is like "pouring money down the drain." (Actually, I do not disagree with them except when I am in the midst of getting into the pool.) They live in a climate that is warm enough for the pool to be tolerable for a few months during the summer.

I always enter my parents' pool the same way. I walk down the steps slowly, trying to ease the painful sensation of being in cold water while fighting the impulse to turn around and get out as the water travels higher up my legs and torso. I think, "Why can't they just heat the pool once in a while?" and then resign myself that I either need to just jump in and get the pain over with in one fell swoop or get out and stop complaining. It takes a little mental convincing, but usually I talk myself into taking a full body plunge into the cool water. It feels momentarily unpleasant and a bit painful, but then I am relieved and refreshed. The next time I get in the pool, I repeat the same process of trying to avoid pain by wading in slowly only to realize after a few minutes that just diving in is a better solution.

I find making the transition to academic work to be similar. The first few months I was writing this book, I would start each writing session by first doing all kinds of unrelated writing tasks and then tasks related but extraneous to writing. First, I checked my e-mail, returned phone calls, paid bills, made tea, and snacked. Then I would wade into writing by fiddling with my outline, reading other dissertation books (and panicking that I have nothing new or important to say), organizing my desk, and editing previous writing. I rationalized to myself, "Alison, you are working on your book even if you are not writing."

On a summer visit to my parents' home while I was working on this book, it occurred to me that all of these work habits were my way of "wading into cool water." I was making the experience of writing more painful by engaging in peripheral activity instead of "jumping in," however uncomfortable that might have been. I began striving to start writing sessions by jumping right into a specific section or subsection. For me, it takes a burst of energy not that dissimilar to the will translated into action that gets me to jump into my parents' pool. I push myself to jump into my work despite feeling unsure of myself. It is painful for a bit, but then I get warmed up and actually forget it was hard to get started. You can finish your dissertation by wading into your work, but it is likely to take much longer than if you find a way to develop a habit of jumping in and more readily make the transition to taking action. So practice jumping in to your dissertation work. It is not easy but with consistent practice, you will get better at more quickly making the transition.

The next summer I visited my parents again and the pool was its usual 78 to 80 degrees. I must have aged that year or experienced some other physiological change because getting in the pool was almost unbearable. No self-coaxing or pleading from my daughter to swim with her could convince me to get in the pool. A few days into my visit, my father came home from work sharing some pool wisdom from a coworker. She told him you could create your own solar panels by covering hula hoops in black garbage bags. You float them in the pool and they absorb the heat from the sun thereby heating the water. On hearing this news, I immediately grabbed the keys to my parents' car and went off to purchase the necessary supplies. In less than 1 hour, assembly was completed and I was ready to begin my solar experiment. Forty-eight hours later, the pool was a wonderful 85 degrees. There was no need to hesitate; I could just jump into the pool without pause. Shortly after this hula hoop–garbage bag miracle, it occurred to me that using strategies to warm up the "writing" pool was at the heart of what I typically did to help students write. As a coach, I was constantly figuring out how to create "writing solar panels" to make the transition to writing easier.

You may also want to consider how you can warm up the writing pool so that jumping in is easier. Creating timelines and action plans so that your work is broken down into small chunks as discussed in chapters 4 and 5 can certainly warm up the pool. Other ways my clients and I have discovered to warm up the pool are visualizing yourself writing and being productive prior to a given work session (much like a runner might visualize an important race beforehand), having another person hold you accountable for completing a certain amount of work for the day, using the 15-minute rule, getting set up the night before a writing session, planning small actions to start the day, managing and maintaining an organized work environment, and keeping reasonable expectations of the quality and quantity of your writing in a given time. As you aim to more readily make the transition into productive work sessions, I encourage you to notice what strategies and factors seem to warm up or cool off the pool. Over time, you can become more effective at warming up the pool, making it easier to jump in and write.

Pushing Through

There are times when you may find that using all the strategies discussed in this chapter will fail. These are the times when you are just stuck and do not know what next step to take or how to get going. Getting truly stuck does not happen often, but when it does, it is easy to panic. I have found that these stuck times require additional strategies, such as the ones discussed in this section.

GET A SECOND OPINION

Often when students are struggling with their dissertation, they struggle alone at home, in the library, and in their office writing in circles, reading more and more research material, hoping for inspiration, avoiding their work, and becoming demoralized. As a consequence of the solitary nature of working on a dissertation, students often rely solely on their own thoughts and ideas to write, develop, and carry out their study and to deal with research problems and challenges. Most students will get stuck, experience writer's block, or become uncertain about what to write or what action to take at some point. Yet when you feel stymied, you do have a choice. You can stick it out and struggle on your own, or you can seek support and talk things over with another person.

When my clients are struggling, I recommend that they talk with fellow students (current or former), their faculty advisor, or other faculty or committee members. Who you choose to talk with about the challenges you are facing will depend on your comfort level and who is best suited to the particular issues you need to discuss. If you are not sure, start with a student or former student from your department. You may also want to consider forming or joining a dissertation-writing group where you can discuss your work and solicit input from other students.

I remember a time when I was struggling a great deal with making a major revision to my dissertation literature review. For my final dissertation, I needed to do some new writing as well as substantially revise, reorganize, and reconceptualize the literature review I had written as part of my proposal, and I had developed a major case of writer's block. After I had struggled for several months, a wise professor pointed out to me that writer's block is really a thinking block and that my problem was that I could not figure out how to think differently about my literature review by myself.

After this conversation, I asked a friend and fellow student, Bernadette, if I could get her input on my literature review challenges. I met Bernadette at a coffee shop and brought a print out of the latest (and quite convoluted) version of my literature review. I laid it out on the table and basically gave her a tour of what I had written, what I was trying to do, and my organizational and conceptual dilemmas. She occasionally reflected back what she heard me saying and made a few suggestions. Actually, she did not need to say much. By the end of the meeting, I had developed a substantially improved mental outline of how to revise and organize the literature review just from talking out loud about my struggles. I went home that afternoon and spent several hours cutting, pasting, editing, and doing new writing. By day's end, I had substantially revised and improved my literature review.

After months of struggle, I was quite amazed at how helpful my meeting with Bernadette proved to be. What struck me most was how the meeting was less about having Bernadette solve my literature review problems for me than it was about the opportunity to talk with someone instead of writing and thinking alone. It was the chance to process my ideas and dilemmas verbally that made the difference. Talking through research and writing issues can considerably enhance your ability to think through complex ideas and determine an organization strategy, and it can improve your ability to articulate and express yourself. The next time you are struggling with your writing, consider talking it over with someone else. The person does not necessarily need to be knowledgeable in your research area unless you need substantive advice and input. Often just having someone listen helps you process and think through important ideas.

Of course, you may struggle with other issues, such as the selection of a topic, the development of a sound conceptual framework, the design of your study, or data analysis. When you are experiencing such challenges, you would likely benefit from finding someone who is knowledgeable and approachable to discuss your area of concern. Resist the temptation to struggle alone. Solitary struggle does not make you nobler or make your dissertation more worthy than the dissertation of someone who sought help. I recommend that you list several people (see Exercise 6.1) who are good resources for discussing dissertation challenges and add them to the bottom of your dissertation timeline. The next time you are struggling, plan a meeting with someone from your list. You are likely to benefit from the support.

READ OTHER DISSERTATIONS

A common reason that graduate students struggle to be productive is that they have little sense of what a dissertation is supposed to look like. Often, reading defended dissertations by other people in your own department can provide you with a better sense of what a dissertation looks like and a general sense of what is expected. You can ask former students for copies of their dissertation. Also, most libraries and even departments keep bound copies of students' dissertations on file. At the time I wrote my master's thesis (a qualitative study), I found it very helpful to review a former student's qualitative dissertation study, especially her method section, to get an idea of what I would need to write. Her dissertation study was quite different from my project, but I was able to use it as an example to get started.

Exercise a bit of caution when using this strategy. When you read someone else's dissertation in its final, bound form, you are reading material that has likely been through many rounds of revisions on the

---

EXERCISE 6.1

List people who are good resources to discuss dissertation challenges:

_____

_____

_____

_____

_____

_____

_____

basis of feedback from others and that has required considerable time, effort, and struggle to take shape. If you find yourself becoming anxious and wondering how you will do a dissertation at the level you are reading, remind yourself that this dissertation was not written in a day or even a month and likely involved much sustained effort. It is possible that you will read other people's dissertations and have the opposite experience. Sometimes, students find it reassuring to see that most dissertations are not prize-winning or publication ready. Reading other people's dissertations can be a way to recalibrate your expectations and see that your dissertation does not need to be a magnum opus.

TEAM UP

One way to overcome writing blocks is to use the buddy system, in which you plan to work in the presence of another person, either someone who is also stuck and needs help or someone who is working productively and can be a role model for you. When you work with another person, you may feel a sense of social pressure to work and are likely to find it easier to focus your attention on the work you need to complete. Many of my clients find it helpful to set up specific, regular times to work alongside a fellow graduate student. If you choose to use the buddy system, make sure you set some ground rules about talking and socializing during the work session. For example, agreed-on breaks after a certain amount of time can be used as motivators and rewards. Many of my clients meet their buddy at the library, where talking is discouraged. When used well, the buddy system can be a great way to increase your motivation and progress on your dissertation.

WRITE JUST A FEW SENTENCES MORE

As you are working on your dissertation, you will likely encounter moments that seem to occur out of the blue when suddenly you do not feel like working another minute. This desire to stop working is often fueled by fatigue, boredom, anxiety, or a feeling of inadequacy. In those moments, see whether you can push through and do something such as write a few more sentences, enter a little more data, or read another paragraph. Many of my clients have developed a "push through" habit that involves writing at least a few more sentences or moving on to another topic, outline point, or section when the drive to write seems to wind down.

My clients tell me that they are often surprised by their ability to write more than they expected and the desire to stop working passes. Somehow the act of writing just a little bit more helps them move past the momentary desire to do something else. If you are honestly at a point where your energy and focus for dissertation work are expended, then it is of course okay to stop. It may even be important to stop as a way to preserve your energy for the next day of work (Bolker, 1998).

If you decide to stop writing, then I recommend that you write some notes to yourself about where you are ending and where you want to pick up your work the next day.

Strategies for Dealing With the Revision Process

When you finish writing a chapter or your entire first draft, you may rightfully feel a sense of accomplishment. Yet at this point the idea of revising may be quite unappealing. After all that intensive thinking and writing, you may feel physically, mentally, and emotionally exhausted. This is natural. If you can, plan a break at this point; a week away from your dissertation can be ideal, but even a 3- or 4-day weekend can help. Do not think about your dissertation during this time, and have fun as a way of celebrating what you have accomplished so far. View this break as a time to refuel. When you return to your dissertation, consider the strategies discussed in this section that can help you to complete this next stage of the dissertation process.

CONSIDER THE EXCITING PARTS OF REVISING

For most students, revising the dissertation is much easier than writing the first draft. Many find it fun or exciting to develop their ideas further, polish their prose, and even explore new territory. Bolker (1998) wrote that "one of the best kept writing secrets is that the more you revise, the clearer, more fluid and more natural your writing will be" (p. 116). Watching rough sentences become polished is rewarding. When you begin each revision session, take advantage of these rewards by rereading a page or two of the elegant writing you produced through your revision work in the last session. This may motivate you to continue revising.

REVISE WITH A PLAN

I coach students to use three concrete strategies in their revision plan. They have reported to me that these strategies seem self-evident once they hear them but that they were often so overwhelmed at the beginning of the revision process that they had not been able to think of them. The first strategy is to print a hard copy of your entire dissertation, paginated consecutively at either the top or bottom of the page. Many students try to revise their dissertation while scrolling up and down a computer screen. This approach may work well if you are revising individual sentences or paragraphs. But if you are trying to reorganize a chapter or make fairly substantial revisions, it is usually better to have a printed copy so you can lay pages out side by side and see larger parts of your dissertation instead of just one page at a time.

Second, if your revisions are substantial or based on someone else's feedback, it is a good idea to first make an inventory of the changes you will need to make before launching into the revisions. Usually feedback consists of editing and substantive suggestions. On the basis of this feedback, you can create a "revision inventory," or an itemized list of the changes needed. Your first inventory item is to do all of the recommended line editing (spelling, grammar, rephrasing, or cutting of sentences). You do not need to list an inventory item for each line edit. Next, list each suggested substantive change as an individual item. For example, if the person reviewing your dissertation commented on page 2 of your draft that you need to add more literature to a particular paragraph or strengthen a certain aspect of your argument, you would note that task as your second inventory item. If the reviewer states that your description of a particular study is confusing and needs clarification, you would note this needed change as your third inventory item.

Read through the entire document until you have catalogued all of the feedback, noting any questions you have for the person reviewing your dissertation regarding the feedback. You can also read your dissertation yourself and create a revision inventory on the basis of your own instincts about what substantive changes you think you need to make. Either type of inventory is something you can readily use when you make your action plan for a given week. You can assign specific inventory items to specific days so that the revision process is more systematic and feels more doable. I have found that my clients who consistently make these kinds of inventories make their revisions in a timelier manner and are better able to handle feedback. Usually when you face the feedback directly, you will see that it is not as harsh or as impossible to address as it may have seemed at first glance.

A third strategy is to read your work and deconstruct it in some way. Graduate students often tell me that revising their work feels overwhelming. What I suggest to students is that they do a "deconstruction" of their most recent draft. This deconstruction consists of reading the draft to determine what has been written, what seems out of place, what seems to be missing, what is worth keeping as is, and what needs substantial revision or reorganization. Many of my clients create a reverse outline in which they outline what has already been written. This outline does not need to be formal. It could simply be a list of subject headings, points being made under each subject heading and notes about what is missing, confusing, disorganized, and so forth. Part of this deconstruction can also involve making notes to yourself about further reading you need to do and questions or dilemmas you would like to discuss with others. Creating a reverse outline can be a very helpful strategy to help you develop a new outline of how you want to revise your existing work. In addition, Bolker (1998) made a couple of other good suggestions about making revisions. One, she recommended reading your work out loud to hear how it sounds. Two, she suggested deliberately reading your work with the aim of simplifying sentences, being more direct, and reducing your use of jargon. However you go about making revisions, keep strategizing to find the approach or approaches that work best for you.

CONSIDER HIRING AN EDITOR

Over the years many of my clients have hired editors to help them refine their writing. For some students, knowing that their dissertation will be professionally edited at a future point makes the task of writing on any given day easier and actually helps them be more productive in that they do not need to obsess over every sentence and worry whether their grammar, sentence structure, and formatting are perfect. It can also be reassuring to know that someone else is reading your dissertation to see if it flows and makes sense. Working with an editor can be especially helpful for students who are nonnative English speakers and may have particular concerns about their ability to write and express themselves clearly and accurately in English. An editor cannot write your dissertation for you, but he or she can help you improve the readability of your dissertation and improve your confidence in the final product. Naturally, check with your university to ensure that their guidelines allow use of an editor.

There are different types of editors who edit doctoral dissertations. Some editors focus on the mechanics of writing, such as spelling, grammar, sentence structure, flow, readability for the target audience, and format consistency. Others also focus on developmental editing and the overall organization of your work. Such editors may point out areas of writing that are difficult to understand, require more background information or development, or seem disorganized. They may also point out where your argument is weak or inconsistent. In my opinion, good editors do some or all of the above but do not offer ghostwriting services. Doctoral students bear the responsibility to be the authors of their work. Having any other person write your dissertation for you is unethical and violates your academic responsibility.

You can learn a lot about writing from an editor. Look for an editor who is willing to help you understand the rationale for his or her suggested changes. In this way, your work with an editor can help you improve your writing skills. Seek an editor who has experience editing dissertations or academic writing in your field, who is an expert in using the appropriate formatting required by your university (e.g., APA or Chicago style), and who is willing to offer references. I highly recommend checking references and calling several editors to find the best person to meet your needs. Editors charge by the hour, the page, or the project. It is reasonable to expect an estimate of the cost of editing your dissertation. You may want to give the editor a few pages to edit so you can see the quality of the work before you agree to work with him or her.

Many students work long hours trying to make the dissertation match their university's formatting guidelines. If you do plan to hire an editor, focus on the content rather than the format of your dissertation, because your formatting work will duplicate work the editor will do. Your editor can quickly set up formatting that will be robust and comprehensive, including pagination and automatically generated tables of contents and figures. Additionally, he or she can format citations and references for style and consistency.

If paying for a dissertation editor is not in your budget, see if you can find another student with whom you can trade editing. Remember, no matter who has edited your dissertation, you are ultimately responsible for the content and quality of your work. Once you receive an edited version of your dissertation, be certain to review it carefully for errors, inaccuracies, and editing that may have changed the meaning of your sentences.

Acknowledge Yourself

Until you reach the end of your dissertation there is always more work to do and the next action to complete. It is easy to focus on what you need to do or what you failed to do and forget to acknowledge yourself for what you have accomplished along the way. Until you submit your dissertation for review, few people, if any, are aware of the day-to-day work you do or the times you pushed through and worked when you did not feel like it. There is no built-in external reward system inspiring you to keep going. Yet, no matter how much dissertation work remains, the small accomplishments along the way deserve to be acknowledged. When you pat yourself on the back and give yourself credit for your hard work, you are likely to feel more motivated to keep working. Some of my clients actually write a statement like "acknowledge myself for a job well done" as the last action for a given day or week as a reminder to celebrate their accomplishments.

The strategies discussed in this chapter can go a long way toward improving your ability and motivation to write and work consistently on your dissertation. To complete your dissertation, you also need to build and maintain good working relationships with your dissertation chairperson and committee. Chapter 7 offers your sounds strategies to build, enhance, and maintain these critical relationships.

Working With Your Dissertation Chairperson and Committee   7

A good working relationship with your dissertation chairperson and committee can go a long way toward making your dissertation experience a positive one. In this chapter, I discuss ways in which these working relationships can best be established, enhanced, and managed for optimal success in completing your dissertation. I describe five strategies for working well with your chairperson, which also apply to working with your committee. Then I describe strategies for successful proposal and dissertation defense meetings, which involve both your committee and your chairperson. Finally, I describe strategies for revising your work after these meetings.

How to Work Well With Your Chairperson

Like any important relationship, your relationship with your chairperson will require sustained care and attention. This is especially important considering the roles the chairperson may play in completing your dissertation and in your graduate career. For example, if you encounter a serious problem with your research or are in danger of being asked to leave your program for some reason, having a chairperson who believes in you may be the only factor that saves you from a premature exit from graduate school. Even if you do not encounter any major hurdles, a good relationship with your chairperson will make it an easier road to the PhD finish line.

In addition to maintaining a good relationship with your chairperson, it is also important to realize that creating and maintaining this relationship is much more your responsibility than it is your chairperson's. Dissertation chairs have other major responsibilities and priorities that vie for their time and attention. If you have chosen your chairperson wisely, your dissertation may be important to your chair, but the relationship aspects of working together will not be his or her focus. Therefore, the biggest contribution you can make to having a good and productive working relationship with your chairperson is to take responsibility for managing the relationship. Fortunately, this will not be that difficult if you use the strategies described in this chapter.

CLARIFY MUTUAL EXPECTATIONS

First and foremost, clarify your mutual expectations of working together. You may already have a sense of your chairperson's expectations of you as a student, yet it is worth directly clarifying these expectations. Such clarification can go a long way toward building a good working relationship. Start by seeking to understand your responsibilities as a graduate student in the eyes of your department or university. Most departments or universities have a dissertation handbook that usually specifies department norms and expectations regarding dissertations and working with faculty. It is a good idea to review this handbook before beginning your dissertation and perhaps again as reminder when you are in the midst of the project. Your chairperson will likely appreciate working with a student who is knowledgeable of the dissertation handbook.

You will also benefit from understanding the specific and perhaps unique expectations of your chairperson. Here are some questions you may want to use as a guide as you clarify your chairperson's expectations:

1. Does your chairperson prefer that you deliver drafts via e-mail, printed copies, or both?
2. Is your chairperson willing to look at rough drafts and give you comments or does he or she prefer more polished, well-developed drafts?
3. Does your chairperson want to see chapters individually or wait until you have several to turn in all at once?
4. How much time does your chairperson typically need to give you feedback?
5. What should you do if you have waited longer than the expected interval of time for feedback?

6. How does your chairperson want you to handle a deadline that you miss?
7. What is your chairperson's preferred means of communication with you (e-mail, phone) to set up meetings, handle questions, and so forth?
8. Does your chairperson prefer to meet during office hours or scheduled meetings outside of office hours?
9. How does your chairperson want you to communicate with other committee members? Does your chairperson prefer to be notified before you schedule meetings with committee members or does he or she feel comfortable with your independently soliciting their feedback and input?

Ask these questions of your chairperson as you deem appropriate. Even if you think you know the answers, you may be making assumptions about your chairperson's expectations and would be better off asking for direct clarification. You may want to talk with other advisees of your chairperson to learn about his or her expectations of students and what they think is critical to working well the particular faculty member. Other advisees may have useful knowledge about your chairperson's expectations as well as tips and strategies that will promote a positive advisor–advisee relationship.

You may also want to communicate your expectations of your chairperson. For example, you may be working with specific time constraints because of a department deadline, need to collect data in a specific window of time, or have a strong desire to finish your dissertation by a certain date for personal or professional reasons. Consequently, you may need his or her support to propose or finish your dissertation by that date. It is up to you to clearly communicate those time constraints to your chairperson. I caution you against pressuring your chairperson to meet your expectations. Make a request and provide a rationale for that request, but then recognize that you cannot force or rigidly demand that your chair agree to your time frame.

In addition, I recommend that you give thought to what you hope for or need from your chairperson to make the relationship work well. Is there a certain way you prefer feedback? Do you hope to meet at regular intervals? It is okay to clarify what you are hoping for in the relationship. It is important, though, to be flexible with your expectations. Your chairperson may not be willing to oblige, and because you need your chairperson to earn your degree, you will need to find a way to work within his or her constraints.

BE PROFESSIONAL

A key means of developing and maintaining a good working relationship with your chairperson is to conduct yourself and the processes involving your dissertation in a professional manner. By being professional, you show your advisor that you take the commitment to doing a dissertation and earning a doctoral degree seriously. You also increase the odds that your chairperson will behave professionally when it comes to advising and supervising your work. Being professional means that you conduct yourself as a mature adult who is respectful of your chairperson, his or her time, and the responsibility it is to oversee your dissertation. A key avenue to maintain an attitude of respect and appreciation is to consider how behavior would be seen from your advisor's point of view (which is likely different than your own). Would it be viewed as professional? If the answer is no, or if you are uncertain, reconsider your behavior before you act, acknowledge and apologize for any past unprofessional behavior, and commit to changing your ways in the future. Some specific points for consideration as you strive to conduct yourself in a professional manner are how you handle meetings, deadlines, the quality of drafts you turn in to your chairperson, and how you respond to the feedback you receive from your chairperson.

Meetings

When it comes to meetings, respect your chairperson's time. Avoid being late to meetings, missing meetings, or canceling at the last minute unless you have a real emergency. It is important to come to meetings prepared and ready to engage in a meaningful interaction. I encourage students to write a list of questions or talking points prior to meetings so they can make good use of the time, demonstrate their professionalism, and increase the likelihood of receiving the input and feedback they need. Make sure you schedule and coordinate proposal and defense meetings yourself. Do not expect your chairperson to do this for you.

Deadlines

Whether you, your chairperson, or your department sets them, deadlines are something to take seriously. If you miss a deadline or know you will miss one, make sure you are up-front by acknowledging it and clearly communicating when you will complete the work. Such communication will demonstrate your professionalism and give you the added benefit of helping you feel more accountable.

Quality of Drafts

Do your best to turn in drafts of your work that you have proofread and revised to ensure quality writing and a clean draft. Many faculty members have told me that they feel frustrated and unmotivated to read their students' work when it has not been proofread. If you need help with your writing, obtain assistance from an editor, a peer you can trust in your program, or the university writing center. Do not expect your advisor to be your editor. I am not suggesting that you need to turn in perfect drafts or even near-perfect drafts. Just make sure you submit drafts that have been read for clarity, edited, and proofread. If you have specific questions, concerns, or unresolved issues in your work, embed notes about them in the document or note them in a cover letter that you include with your draft. Communicating unresolved issues helps your chairperson focus on giving you feedback that is most useful to you. There is one caveat about cover letters that is worth mentioning. Sometimes a cover letter acknowledging questions and concerns you have about your work is interpreted by faculty members as indicative that the draft is incomplete, and therefore they will not be willing to read the draft. If your advisor is only willing to provide feedback on complete, well-developed drafts, you may want to avoid cover letters noting questions and concerns. Instead, do your best to solicit answers to questions and dilemmas via discussion with your advisor or other people that will help your address these issues before you submit you work.

Feedback

In the interest of being professional and doing quality work, it is very important to be open to your advisor's feedback, maintain a nondefensive stance, and be willing to address the feedback. If you do not agree with the feedback, work with your advisor to explain your point of view, but make sure that in the process you somehow acknowledge his or her point of view. Keep your eye on the bigger goal of finishing your dissertation, and be willing to compromise in the interest of getting to the finish line. Do not compromise your values or agree to do work that is inaccurate, substandard, or completely outside your area of interest. But do be willing to consider that your advisor has wisdom, knowledge, and experience that informs his or her ideas about how to improve your work and make it acceptable to your committee and worthy of a PhD.

It is critical to remember that feedback on your academic work is exactly that, feedback on your academic work. It is not commentary on your worth as a human being. Monitor your own response to feedback and be on the lookout for negative beliefs that rear their head and contribute to feeling personally attacked, depressed, angry, or worthless. It is easy to listen to critical feedback as criticism instead of as a critique. Remind yourself that your advisor is likely protecting you from problems down the road and increasing your odds of having a successful dissertation experience. Feedback may hurt your feelings, make you angry, or make you want to retreat from your dissertation for a while. At some point, though, you will need to move forward and address your advisor's input and suggestions and handle the feedback you receive in a professional manner.

There are occasions when a dissertation advisor gives feedback in a way that is unduly harsh or even abusive. These incidents are rare, but they can be extremely damaging when they do occur. If your chairperson (or a committee member) insults your intelligence, gives feedback with very little constructive content, or expresses excessively harsh sentiments about you or your work, I recommend that you first reach out to someone else. You likely need a reality check to help you determine what parts of the feedback are fair and what parts are harsh or unreasonable. Talk with a peer and then a faculty member you trust about what you can do to address the feedback. Sometimes feedback seems harsher in writing than intended by your chairperson because written notes do not adequately convey tone. Also, some advisors neglect positive feedback so their critique seems callous or cruel in the absence of anything positive. I encourage you to consider whether the problem is more style than substance. In other words, consider whether your chairperson truly intends to be cruel or rather lacks good social skills and sensitivity when delivering critiques of students' work.

After receiving what seems like very harsh feedback, I suggest you set up a meeting to discuss it. In such a meeting, strive to remain professional and see whether you can obtain more constructive information about what you will need to do to improve your work. On several occasions, I have witnessed students receive very harsh criticism in writing. Yet when the student had an in-person meeting to discuss the feedback, their advisor was much kinder and more constructive. Do your best to stay calm and hear the feedback without letting it hijack your nervous system and make you feel worthless. Listen for the kernels of useful feedback among any harsh or critical statements. If you feel strongly that you are being bullied or verbally abused in some way by your chairperson, you may need to involve another committee member or even the chair of your department. You may even need another committee person to act as an "unofficial chairperson." Handling such a scenario requires a delicate hand but may be a better avenue than trying to change your dissertation advisor mid-course. If it comes down to changing to a different chairperson, it is best if you can find a supportive faculty person in your department who will advocate the change on your behalf.

If you do involve other faculty members in your department, it may help if you have documented the communication between you and your chairperson so you can demonstrate the problems you are experiencing. Make sure you do not exaggerate what is happening when communicating with others. When stating your case, avoid insulting your chairperson's character, giving your interpretation of your chairperson's feedback, or talking about how it made you feel. Rather, be professional and stick to the facts of what was said and written by your chairperson regarding your dissertation. Otherwise you risk looking like you are exaggerating, emotionally unstable, and the source of the problem.

BE PROACTIVE

I encourage you to take a proactive stance when it comes to working with your chairperson. Being proactive means that you take charge of your dissertation and demonstrate your active engagement in the project. You are not waiting for your chairperson to give you the answers, do the work for you, or push you to do the work. When you are proactive, you recognize that it is up to you to initiate meetings with your chairperson and have a clear agenda for those meetings. Make it a point to meet on a regular basis so your chairperson is aware of your progress and has more opportunities to mentor and advise you. When you show up to a meeting, be polite but know what you want out of a meeting. Gently guide the meeting in the direction you want it to go. You will get more value from the meeting if you show up ready to be engaged and interactive. If you are having problems with your dissertation, be proactive and take the initiative to identify one or more possible solutions to a problem rather than hoping your advisor will offer a solution to you. Thank your chairperson for meeting with you and take clear action to move your dissertation forward between meetings. Chairpersons are generally more engaged when you consistently make progress because there is a sense of action and direction to your dissertation work.

A common problem that requires students to maintain a positive, proactive stance is dealing with a long wait to receive feedback on a submitted draft. A reasonable amount of time to wait for feedback will range, depending on your field of study, department norms, the work submitted, and the workload of your chairperson. Typically in the social, life, and physical sciences I have seen faculty take 1 to 4 weeks to give feedback while students in the humanities often but not always wait longer (1–2 months or more). If you submit a chapter or a shorter portion of your dissertation, it is reasonable to expect a faster turnaround time provided your chairperson does not happen to be on sabbatical, in the midst of applying for a major grant, or otherwise overloaded with work. If you clarify what typical turnaround times are with your chairperson, you will be better able to gauge when your wait is atypically long.

I have coached many doctoral students whose chairpersons took an excessively long time to provide feedback on complete or partial drafts of their dissertations. These students often express frustration and disappointment at the slow turnaround time. If you have been waiting a long time for feedback, do your best to maintain a positive, proactive stance toward the situation. Rather than be consumed by anger and frustration, strategize how you can make the situation better. For example, some clients specifically schedule a meeting to discuss the latest submitted draft instead of waiting for feedback before they schedule the follow-up meeting. Faculty members are busy people who often need a meeting to give them a sense of urgency and accountability to read their students' work. I have witnessed many students successfully use the strategies of sharing their dissertation timelines with their chairperson, writing clear cover notes requesting specific input and feedback, or writing a diplomatic but assertive e-mail regarding the status of the feedback to shorten turnaround time. For example:

> Dr. Smith,
>
> I wanted to check in and see if you had a chance to read the latest draft of my dissertation submitted to you on May 15. I know this is a busy time of year so I want to be respectful of your other time commitments. If possible, I would like to set up a meeting with you to discuss the latest draft I submitted. I look forward to your feedback and appreciate your time and attention to my dissertation.
>
> Thank you.

Sometimes, no matter how proactive and assertive you are, receiving feedback in a timely manner, if at all, is difficult. If lack of feedback, no matter your effort to receive it, is a problem, stop and consider if the quality of the work you are submitting is part of the problem. Perhaps your work is full of typographical errors, grammar mistakes, and awkward, hard to understand sentences and paragraphs. Maybe your ideas and argument are confusing and convoluted. If your work is sub par, your chairperson may delay reviewing it because it requires so much energy and effort to read. Long waits for feedback could, of course, occur for a large variety of other reasons that have nothing to do with the quality of your work, such as the workload of your chairperson or other doctoral students vying for his or her attention.

What are your options when feedback seems impossible to obtain? You can solicit feedback from other committee members with whom you have a good relationship. Be careful not to upset your chairperson by going to other faculty members. Let your chairperson know that you would like to solicit feedback from another committee person, and, if your chairperson objects, it is a good idea to respect the objections. You may try talking with other students who work with the chairperson or even the chair of your department about how you can effectively deal with the lack of feedback and responsiveness of your chairperson. In the worst-case scenario (which I would avoid unless it is the absolute last resort), I have seen students go to a proposal or a defense meeting with little feedback from their chairperson or committee. Thus, the defense meeting becomes the setting where the student receives feedback. Usually, revisions (sometimes significant) are then made after the defense meeting. Such a scenario is not only less than ideal it can be risky. Yet it may be your only way to receive feedback if everything else you have tried has failed. For the vast majority of students, maintaining a positive, proactive relationship with your chairperson will facilitate the process of obtaining timely and regular feedback on their dissertations.

Your advisor has wisdom and power, and it is up to you to find a way to work as well as possible together. Even if it is challenging to have a good working relationship with your advisor, you will need to find a way to make the best of the situation. Talk with other students or trusted faculty members about how to improve the situation. Avoid gossiping and complaining about your advisor. Instead, aim to talk about the relationship difficulties with the intention of finding a solution or strategy to move things forward. Be proactive and creative and keep your eyes on the ultimate goal of earning your degree to motivate you to overcome relationship challenges.

TAKE RESPONSIBILITY FOR YOUR DISSERTATION

When it comes to working well with your advisor, it is important that you take responsibility for your dissertation. This advice may sound quite obvious, but I have witnessed many students who struggled to take true responsibility for their work. Consequently, their relationship with their chairperson faltered and they struggled to make consistent progress. Taking responsibility means that you understand that you are the cause of what is or is not happening with your dissertation. Whether you are making consistent progress or struggling to be productive and make your dissertation a priority, you are responsible for the outcome. Now, I can hear your objections already. You may be thinking of all of the external issues that are outside of your control: delays obtaining human participants approval, difficulty accessing primary or secondary sources, committee members who are not getting along, data collection delays, or an unresponsive chairperson. You are correct that there are situations that can be outside your immediate control. At the same time, you are responsible for how you respond to such difficulties. You can choose to maintain a flexible attitude and keep looking for ways to impact the situation in a positive way or you can choose to blame your difficulties on other people or circumstances. When you blame others or your circumstances, you lose the power to be effective in the face of adversity. You become a victim and lose sight of what you can do to improve the situation. Taking responsibility for your dissertation means that you are willing to take ownership of how your dissertation is and is not moving forward. You understand that you are at the helm and that your progress and your response to challenges are up to you.

It is also your responsibility to do the actual work of your dissertation. Despite the apparent nature of this statement, I have encountered many clients who harbored the wish that their advisor would give them answers and tell them what they should do. Usually, these desires stem from the student's fear that they are not up to the challenge themselves. They become uncomfortable with the struggle and ambiguity in the dissertation process and begin looking outside themselves for answers. At times, I have seen students become frustrated and even angry when their dissertation advisor suggested further reading or directed them to another faculty member instead of giving direct advice or answers of how to revise their work. I can appreciate and understand this frustration. Nonetheless, your dissertation is a critical opportunity for learning and demonstrating your skills, abilities, and competence as a researcher.

As noted in the beginning of this chapter, maintaining a relationship with your chairperson is also your responsibility. I have witnessed many students become disappointed, angry, and discouraged because their chairpersons did not initiate or maintain contact with them. It would be nice if all dissertation advisors made communicating with advisees a priority. Yet faculty have many competing priorities, and it will likely be up to you to take responsibility for initiating and maintaining communication with your chairperson. If it has been a while since you spoke to your chairperson and you have not been actively working on your dissertation, I encourage you to reestablish contact. You need your chairperson to make it to the finish line. Call or e-mail your advisor to acknowledge that you have been out of touch. Let him or her know that you are ready to begin working regularly on your dissertation and that you remain committed to finishing your project. Once you reestablish contact, it is imperative that you demonstrate actual commitment to finishing by turning in drafts, attending meetings with your chairperson, and maintaining regular communication.

Handling the paperwork associated with doing a dissertation also requires you to assume primary responsibility. Over the years, faculty members have complained to me that students routinely show up to their offices with forms they need signed and have not first filled out the forms. In addition, students sometimes wait until the last minute to file for extensions or fill out important paperwork requiring faculty approval and signatures. Plan ahead so your advisor knows what is happening and what paperwork needs to be handled. Make sure you take responsibility for handling all of the documents associated with your dissertation so that they are signed and delivered to the appropriate offices on time.

HAVE REALISTIC EXPECTATIONS OF YOUR CHAIRPERSON AND YOUR COMMITTEE

Maintaining realistic expectations of your advisor will make it easier to establish and maintain a good working relationship. Be aware of any excessive standards or rigid expectations you may have of your chairperson. You are not perfect and neither is your chairperson. Every chairperson has his or her areas of strength and weakness when it comes to advising students. So I encourage you to let go of demands you may have for your dissertation advisor to meet all of your expectations. Look out for rigid expectations you may have such as "My advisor should always read a submitted draft within a week" or "She should just tell me how to fix the problems I am having with my conceptual framework." Also, be on the lookout for overgeneralizing and damning your advisor as discussed in chapter 2 (e.g., "My dissertation advisor was very critical in our last meeting. He is a jerk who does not care about me"). I am not suggesting that you accept bad behavior such as being yelled at, harshly criticized, or ignored. Yet I do encourage you to maintain healthy preferences instead of demands about your chairperson and your working relationship.

Be willing to make trade-offs when it comes to working with your chairperson. Perhaps your chairperson's students take longer to finish their degrees because it takes longer to receive feedback but he or she is extremely supportive and provides a lot of assistance to students in their job search. Maybe your chairperson is very critical and rarely praises you but he or she does read your drafts carefully and give meaningful feedback that helps you improve your work. Do your best to see the positive aspects of working with your chairperson and avoid dwelling on the negative. By dwelling on the negative, you risk becoming pessimistic about improving the situation and believing there is little or no benefit you can receive from your relationship with your advisor. Also, a rigid and negative viewpoint leaves you unable to creatively and effectively identify solutions to overcome challenges because you can only see the situation one way. The more accepting you can be where you acknowledge, "This is who I work with. I need to make the best of it," the easier it will be to benefit from your advisor's strengths and look for ways to compensate where your advisor may fall short. For example, you may need to look to peers and other faculty members to help you with your writing, study design, or obtain the emotional support you need during the dissertation process.

How to Succeed in Committee Dissertation Meetings

Second only to your relationship with your dissertation chairperson is your relationship with the members of your dissertation committee. These relationships typically involve formal meetings, namely the proposal defense meeting and the final defense meeting.

FORMAL MEETINGS

In the majority of cases, doctoral students meet formally with their entire committee before their study is carried out (i.e., the proposal meeting) and after the study is conducted and the dissertation is written (i.e., the final defense meeting). Yet there are some variations depending on the academic department. In some departments there is no proposal meeting, and in some there is no formal defense meeting. Rather, committee members give comments on the proposal or final write-up and students make revisions until the committee is satisfied. Proposal and final defense meetings are often the source of great anxiety and consternation among students. Yet it is actually beneficial to the student to have all of your committee members in the room together, especially in the proposal phase. When everyone is together, there is a better chance that your committee can work together collaboratively to ensure that your study is of sound design and merits a doctoral degree.

Proposal meetings are usually less formal than final defense meetings. Often students provide a brief presentation to their committee outlining their proposal, the purpose of their study, and how they intend to conduct their research. The purpose of proposal defense meetings is for faculty to evaluate your proposed study and determine if it is of sufficient scope and design to merit a PhD. At your proposal defense meeting, your committee will ask you questions about the study's design, central thesis, research questions, conceptual framework, focus of the study (they may want to know why you are leaving something out or suggest that you narrow the focus of the study), and how you will address potential limitations or problems that they foresee. Be ready to hear your committee make suggestions to improve your study (Cone & Foster, 2006). The input you receive at your proposal defense meeting can significantly improve your study, help prevent problems with your research, and make your final dissertation defense a positive, even celebratory experience.

The final defense meeting is generally more formal than the proposal meeting, with students giving a presentation sometimes using audiovisual aids as they would when delivering a conference presentation. Cone and Foster (2006) noted that the major purpose of the final defense meeting is to evaluate your competence as a researcher. The evaluation is based on both the written document and your performance in the defense meeting. Typically you will be asked to explain what you did and what you found as part of your study as well as the meaning of your research. Your committee will want to see that you can discuss your findings or central argument in relationship to existing theory and the findings of other studies in your area (Cone & Foster, 2006).

What I have just described can sound quite daunting and instill fear even in confident students. I encourage students to avoid thinking of the meeting as a "defense" meeting. A faculty member once told me that he prefers the term "demonstration of competence" to defense meeting. When you think of your meeting as a place you need to defend your ideas, you are more likely to become highly anxious, feel the need to be on guard, and maintain a posture where you are waiting to be attacked. Consequently, it becomes harder to accurately hear your committee members' feedback and participate in a lively, meaningful discussion about your research and how it can be improved. Thinking of your proposal and final defense meeting as a demonstration of competence is a way to remind yourself that your job is to justify what you plan to do at your proposal defense and what you have done at your final defense. If your committee does not agree with your justification, then find out why and learn what you can do to address their concerns. Defense meetings are not about defending your worthiness as a human being or knowing everything under the sun that one could possibly know related to your dissertation topic. There are several points of consideration to increase your odds of having a successful proposal or final defense meeting.

WORK CLOSELY WITH YOUR CHAIRPERSON PRIOR TO THE MEETINGS

First, do your best to work well with your advisor and obtain meaningful feedback that you integrate prior to the defense meeting. It is very important that you work closely with your chairperson and seek his or her approval that your proposal or final dissertation is ready to be defended. He or she has usually participated on many dissertation committees and will have a good sense of when you are ready to defend your proposal or final dissertation. If your advisor does not believe you are ready to go to committee, it is best to heed that advice. Keep improving your proposal or final dissertation until your advisor believes you are ready. If you advisor believes you have meaningfully integrated his or her feedback, he or she is much more likely to advocate for you in proposal and final defense meetings.

PREPARE, PREPARE, PREPARE

Another important way to make defense meetings successful is to be well prepared. Find out ahead of time the typical norms for defense meetings in your department. Talk with your advisor about the expectations of your opening presentation. In some programs, a formal 45-minute presentation with audiovisual aids is expected. In other departments, there is a more casual approach to the presentation in terms of length, content, and formality. Also, talk with other students about their experiences, how they prepared, how they successfully participated in the meeting, and any mistakes they made or pitfalls to avoid. When I was in graduate school, my peers and I held mock defense meetings for each other. In these mock defenses, we asked questions of the student defending his or her work as if we were faculty. On many occasions, the questions in the mock defense were harder than the actual defense meeting. Alternatively, you can prepare for defense meetings by talking directly to your chairperson or other students about what you are likely to be asked. It is also important to carefully review your submitted proposal or final dissertation prior to your defense meeting. Have a good handle on what you have written and what you are proposing you will do or what you have done. Mark up a printed copy of your work in a way that makes it is easy for you to find key sections, tables, and figures in case you need to refer to the document during the defense meeting. Up-front preparation for your proposal and final defense meetings can contribute to a much easier experience for you and your committee.

MAINTAIN A NONDEFENSIVE STANCE

Maintaining a nondefensive stance during defense meetings is also extremely important. Do your best to listen to your committee members as people who are asking questions and giving you ideas because they want to help you have the best study possible. Such listening will help you remain nondefensive, hear what they are saying, and respond to their questions and comments thoughtfully. The vast majority of faculty members are on the student's side. They are making comments, asking questions, and giving you feedback because they want you to succeed, not to attack you or make you feel inadequate. Often committee members' questions and recommendations are their way of trying to protect you in the long run from running into problems with your study. It is also your committee's job to assess students and whether they are developing competence as researchers. This assessment is not personal. It is their job.

When faculty members make suggestions or critique your work, your job is hear what they have to say and acknowledge it. Say, for example, "that is an interesting idea" and comment on it in some way that demonstrates you understand their point of view. If you do not understand what the faculty member is saying, it is okay to ask for clarification. If you are asked a difficult question and you do not immediately know the answer, do not panic. Take a deep breath and either ask for a moment to think about the question or ask that the question be restated. Take your time and do your best to focus on answering the question being asked instead of giving a response that is fueled by anxiety that does not actually answer the question. You can also try restating the question as you hear it. Often, restating the question will prompt the committee member to clarify the question or even ask an entirely different question that is much easier to answer.

USE ACTIVE LISTENING AND BE CALM

I always remind my clients to focus on the actual words being said by their committee members rather than their own interpretation of what is being said. For example, when a committee member tells you that he is concerned that a proposed analysis strategy is flawed, he is saying, "I think your proposed analysis strategy is flawed." He is not saying, "I think you are flawed. You'll never get a PhD." One way to listen more accurately to what committee members are saying is to use active listening skills in which you paraphrase back what you hear being said. If a committee member says, "It seems like you have too many independent variables and consequently the study lacks focus," you can mirror back, "So you are saying that you are concerned that my study lacks focus because of the number of independent variables." Active listening can help you stay calm and acknowledge what is actually being said instead of getting lost in your own interpretation. Acknowledging does not mean you agree. Rather, it indicates your respect of the committee member's point of view and demonstrates your maturity. Sometimes, simply acknowledging a committee member's ideas, suggestions, or critique is sufficient, and no additional work will need to be done to address the comments. Think of the ability to actively listen as a good friend; you can bring this ability to both your proposal and final defense meeting, and it will help you stay calm, effectively hear what you committee has to say, and avoid taking feedback personally.

When there are differences of opinion on your committee, do your best to stay calm. Use active listening skills to hear what everyone is saying and work to reach an agreement or determine a process to reach an agreement regarding how the problem or issue can be addressed to everyone's satisfaction. Usually your chairperson will step in and facilitate this process and prevent the meeting from becoming a place of contention, political displays, or a forum for faculty members to work out their personal issues. You may want to talk with your advisor about how to best handle conflict if you anticipate any issues before your proposal or final defense meeting.

Despite your fears and concerns about your proposal and final defense meeting, keep in mind that defense meetings can be thought of as a positive learning experience. The defense meeting can be a place of collaboration where research ideas are discussed, setting the stage for a solid plan of action to finish your dissertation or improve your completed study for future publication. When you can think of committee meetings in this way, it is easier to maintain a less defensive stance and a calmer interior.

REVISING YOUR PROPOSAL AFTER THE PROPOSAL DEFENSE MEETING

A common outcome of a student's dissertation proposal meeting is that the student is required to make some revisions to his or her study plan. The extent of those revisions can vary considerably, but it is important to remember that having to make revisions is commonplace. Do your best to maintain a nondefensive stance when your committee requires you to make changes. Remember that no matter how good your proposal, there are always alternative ways of carrying out a study. Other people's points of view are legitimate. An up-front, productive conversation with your committee at your proposal meeting about potential problems and possible solutions to those problems will increase the odds that your committee will be satisfied with your final dissertation. Cone and Foster (2006) reminded students of the importance of taking careful notes at defense meetings to ensure they will know what changes need to be made after the fact. Before your meeting, find out if you or your advisor will take on that responsibility.

At the end of your proposal meeting, it is a good idea to read the suggested changes out loud to make sure there is agreement regarding the changes and that all of them were recorded. You want to make sure that you, your chairperson, and your committee are all in agreement regarding necessary modifications to the proposal. In the days after the meeting, take the time to thank your committee members for their participation on your committee and their recommendations to improve your study. Include an overview of the changes you will be making on the basis of the meeting. In this way, you create a record of what you have agreed to do to improve your study. Faculty members may not remember their recommendations by the time you get to the final defense meeting. Having a record may help jog their memory and protect you from problems when you defend your dissertation.

It is important to think of your dissertation proposal as essentially a contract between you and your committee. You are making an agreement with them that if you carry out the proposed study to the best of your ability that they will grant you a doctoral degree. You may need to make revisions after your final defense, but it is highly unlikely that you will fail your final defense if you uphold the contract you have created with your committee at the proposal stage. Because the proposal is a contract, it is extremely important that you make sure your committee is agreeing to what you are putting before them. By nailing down all of the details of your proposal so that there is a clear, explicit contract between you and your committee, the road to meeting your committee's expectations of your final dissertation will be much easier. If you have to make substantial changes to your dissertation following your proposal meeting, talk with your advisor about whether it would be wise to have a second committee meeting to make sure everyone is on the same page. I realize having your wisdom teeth pulled without anesthesia may sound more appealing than a second proposal meeting. Yet if there were significant concerns and doubts about your study, it may be wise to bring the committee together again to secure a contract for your dissertation in which everyone involved is in agreement. In the long run, you will be better off making sure that all of your committee members have a shared understanding of your revised proposal and agree that it will be sufficient for you to earn a doctoral degree.

If something significant changes once you begin working on your dissertation (e.g., you need to use an alternative data source; your sample size changes considerably, you change the focus of your research), make sure you communicate the changes to your committee to avoid any final defense meeting surprises. Even if you do not make any significant changes to your dissertation, it is a good idea to keep in touch with your committee members with periodic updates on your progress to keep yourself on their radar and maintain a good relationship with them. Talk with your chair about how and when to make such updates.

REVISING YOUR DISSERTATION AFTER THE DISSERTATION DEFENSE MEETING

It is not uncommon for students to be required to make revisions to their dissertations after the final defense meeting. For example, your committee may require additional data analysis, a change in your approach to analyzing data or secondary sources, additions to your literature review, bolstering of your argument, or a better developed theoretical integration of your findings. My advice for handling this feedback is similar to that for handling revisions after your proposal meeting. In some cases, your committee will agree to sign the formal documents granting you a doctoral degree and leave it up to your chairperson to ensure you make the recommended changes. In other situations, your committee will want to see the revisions and only agree to sign required documents following a satisfactory review of your amended dissertation. Either way, I recommend that you work closely with your advisor to make the necessary revisions. I encourage you to make the revisions as quickly as possible while your defense meeting is fresh in your mind. Seek out support to stay on track so you can bring your dissertation to a close.

How Students Fail

Keep in mind that it is extremely rare for someone to fail a dissertation defense. I have witnessed three specific circumstances that led to a student's failure to pass his or her final defense meeting or being asked to leave the program before scheduling a defense meeting. One, the student never established a sound contract with his or her committee in the form of a solid dissertation proposal agreed on by the committee. Two, the student conducted a study that was significantly different from the contract and did not effectively communicate those changes to the committee. Three, the student failed to fulfill the actual study in the agreed-on time frame. Students are typically entitled to a number of extensions (which varies by university) granting them additional time to complete their dissertation. At some point, students may run out of extension options, and, if their work is not completed by the final extension deadline, they may be precluded from scheduling a defense meeting and forced to exit the program without their doctoral degree. In every case I have witnessed a student fail, the student had a history of problems as a graduate student that started long before the dissertation phase began. They also had poor relationships with their dissertation advisor and committee.

You can avoid these scenarios, especially if you follow the recommendations made throughout this book. When you go into your final defense meeting, remind yourself that the worst-case scenario you will experience is being required to make revisions to your dissertation. I realize you would prefer to avoid making revisions, but you are up to the challenge. If you can make it through years of classes, papers, a master's thesis, comprehensive exams, and proposing and carrying out a dissertation study, then certainly you can handle some revisions required by your committee to earn your doctoral degree. I encourage you to work closely with your chairperson and committee to make sure you understand what changes you are being asked to make. Begin the revision process by making a revision inventory as suggested in chapter 6, and then carefully plan when you will make the revisions using a timeline and weekly action plans.

At your defense meetings and during the entire time you work on your dissertation, it is vital to remember that your chairperson and committee members want you to succeed. The effort you make to develop and maintain good working relationships with them will likely pay off in a more positive dissertation experience and, of course, a doctoral degree. I am confident that you can create and enhance your relationship with your chairperson and committee. The ability to build good working relationships in graduate school will serve you well in your career after your degree is completed.

After focusing in this chapter on how to care for and nurture positive relationships with faculty, it is time to turn your attention to the importance of nurturing yourself as you work on your dissertation. Chapter 8 offers you ideas and advice about how you can take better care of yourself on your dissertation journey.

Taking Good Care of Yourself Along the Way

8

A very important strategy to be successful in the pursuit of a PhD and to enjoy life in the process is finding ways to take care of yourself on an ongoing basis. You need and deserve outlets in your life to experience pleasure and relaxation so that you can reduce stress and give yourself a break from academic endeavors. The ability to sustain the energy and motivation required to complete a dissertation is enhanced considerably when you make self-care a real-life priority. An active practice of taking care of yourself can also help you remember that your dissertation is one aspect of your life, not your entire life. It may be easier to maintain a balanced perspective on your dissertation when you have a life beyond the doors of your graduate program that involves attending to your own needs and desires. In this chapter, you will learn what self-care is and what its benefits are, why it can be so challenging for graduate students to take good care of themselves, and strategies you can use to make self-care a more integral part of your life.

Defining Self-Care

By *self-care* I mean engaging in activities that are pleasurable, relaxing, and restorative, and that make you feel healthy, balanced, and able to handle the challenges of life. I like to think of self-care as being kind and nurturing to yourself for no other reason than because you need and deserve good things in life. Self-care is not an obligation. It is about choosing to emphasize nurturing activities in your life (Domar & Dreher, 2000). Most often self-care looks like action you take on your own behalf. For example, you may spend time with friends, exercise, read a book for pleasure, meditate, or take a nap. Self-care may also look like saying no to activities that exceed what you can reasonably handle, setting better boundaries with friends and family, or creating action plans that allow you to balance your need to be productive with the need for pleasure and relaxation. Yet self-care is not just about what you do. It is a life philosophy and a way of life in which people value the quality of their lives and make themselves and their needs a priority. In this way self-care involves a positive mind-set in which you feel entitled to take care of yourself and see self-care as a vital part of life (Domar & Dreher, 2000).

Why Self-Care May Not Be a Part of Your Life

You may be thinking, "I am a doctoral student. I don't have time for self-care" or "I will start taking better care of myself once I finish my dissertation." I know how busy and demanding life as a graduate student can be. Your dissertation can feel like an overgrown octopus whose tentacles have twisted and entangled their way into every corner of your life. It is easy to put off taking good care of yourself when you are facing the challenge of completing a dissertation. In response to the stress and pressure of graduate school, many students dismiss their own needs for rest and pleasure. They rationalize that they will take a break when they get through their next set of deadlines or even when graduate school comes to an end altogether. Spending more time with friends and family, pursuing hobbies, exercising regularly, improving their diet, and more fully enjoying life come to play second fiddle to graduate school.

It is true that in many ways life is easier when the pressure of graduate school and completing a dissertation is behind you. Yet life will continue to present its share of challenges. After graduate school, you will most likely be busy with the demands of a career and other roles and responsibilities in your life. There will be other major projects and endeavors, and it will be all too easy to continue the habit learned in graduate school of delaying pleasure, relaxation, fun, and joy. I strongly believe that self-care is vital throughout life and that it is especially important during the taxing time of being a doctoral student. Making self-care a priority while you are in graduate school can set the stage for a life in which you make your own needs a priority no matter how busy you are.

On my first day of graduate school, the chair of my department gave a short speech to the new students. He talked about the pursuit of a PhD in psychology and the hard work we would do. He told us that we would find it challenging to have a life outside of graduate school but that it was important to "take a bubble bath once in a while." I remember being disheartened to hear that he believed having an active personal life would be so challenging that we would only have time for the equivalent of an occasional bubble bath. Now I am not 100% certain what he meant by his remarks, but I interpreted his words to mean that I would need to make great personal sacrifice and defer many of my own needs until I earned my degree. In my first semester of graduate school, my sense of entitlement to take great care of myself and experience pleasure quickly dwindled as the demands of academic life mounted.

I did spend time with friends, I went out to dinner and parties, took time to exercise, and engaged in other activities that I found enjoyable. Yet the degree of enjoyment I received from such activities seemed to give way to an unwanted emotion: guilt. When I was out with friends, at the gym, or even in a bubble bath, I usually felt that I "should" be doing academic work and be productive in some way. When I failed to live up these expectations, I felt guilty about my lack of performance. Think about your own experience. Are you able to engage in meaningful downtime without guilt? Or do your feel a sense of pressure to always be working? If you are like most graduate students, you have struggled to take guilt-free time away from academics. You likely have a long list of other academic responsibilities and goals in addition to your dissertation. Thus, no matter how much work you have accomplished in a given day, there is always more work to be done. Under the pressure of demands for accomplishment, the desire for pleasure or your own need for relaxation and peace may go underground, and it becomes normal to feel as though you should always be working.

Consequences of Not Taking Care of Yourself

Lack of self-care can affect your emotional and physical well-being as well as important relationships. Inadequate attention to your needs for self-care can lead to difficulty managing stress, depression, anxiety, and low self-esteem (Domar & Dreher, 1996). Your physical health may also suffer without attention to your need to eat well, exercise, and reduce stress. Excess stress in particular can be harmful to your health because your immune system may become suppressed under stress (Sapolsky, 1994). Beyond your own mental and physical well-being, relationships with friends and family can suffer when you do not take time off from academic endeavors. Friends and family can be especially hurt when they see you engaging in some meaningless procrastination activity when you have previously claimed that your time needs to be dedicated to your dissertation.

When you do not give yourself permission to take time to relax or engage in meaningful downtime, you are likely to find yourself feeling tired, burned out, and bored as you work on your dissertation. Thus, you may procrastinate or stop working on your dissertation as you strive to reduce those negative feelings because your dissertation seems to be the source of those feelings. Typically, when students procrastinate in this way, they engage in activities that do not recharge their energy or motivation. They are more likely to choose an activity that they can easily engage in with little effort, such as surfing the Internet, watching reruns on television, or playing computer games. Most of the time, activities like these do not provide a meaningful, restorative break from your dissertation. Also, when students take unplanned breaks from their work, they often feel guilty about the time off. This guilt neutralizes the potential benefit of activities that they normally enjoy and find restorative.

I recognize that the pressure to be productive in graduate school can make it difficult to wind down and allow yourself time off. Yet the reality is that working without rest can go on for only so long. Even if you do not give yourself permission to take a break, you will eventually take a break anyway. The question is whether that break will help you launch a productive work session or lead to guilt and further procrastination. My hope is that you can learn to take more purposeful, planned breaks from your dissertation that help you feel rested, restored, and ready to work when that break comes to an end.

The Dissertation Marathon

If you were an Olympic athlete training to run the marathon and you told me your coach's strategy to help you win the gold medal was to train every single day and never rest, I would tell you to find a new coach. Elite marathon runners know that rest and taking excellent care of themselves is critical to optimal performance. They risk overuse injuries, exhaustion, illness, and suboptimal performance if they do not adequately rest and take care of themselves as part of their training.

There is a parallel truth for those of us in the academic world. Purposeful and meaningful rest, relaxation, and self-care activity are vital to motivation and optimal academic performance. You can only tax your brain with intellectual activity for so long. Having time when your brain can be offline will likely help you work better when it is time to engage in academic endeavors. I often find that some of my best ideas arise when I am at rest. Just like an elite athlete, if you are willing to take real downtime, you may actually perform better. Giving yourself some freedom and space from academic work may be exactly what you need to be successful.

What to Expect at First

Your initial efforts to engage in self-care may not immediately lead to more relaxation, rejuvenation, or productivity. Think of self-care as you would exercise: One trip to the gym does not make you physically fit. Like exercise, obtaining the full benefit from self-care requires consistent practice and effort over time. Even if you go through the motions and do not immediately experience any benefits, you will eventually. In time, you will find that you can more fully wind down, relax, enjoy the moment, and experience pleasure for pleasure's sake. It can take time to restore your ability to relax and let go of the drive to always be accomplishing something. The more you practice, the better you will become at deliberately taking time off from academic work and the quality of the work you do will likely benefit from this time you take for yourself.

You may be reading this chapter and agreeing in principle with what I am saying. Yet you cannot envision how you will start to make self-care more of a life priority. It can certainly feel difficult and even overwhelming to contemplate how to meaningfully relax and rejuvenate. I offer you five strategies to better incorporate self-care activities into your life as you seek to complete your doctoral dissertation.

STRATEGY 1: GIVE YOURSELF THE ROLE OF SELF-NURTURER IN YOUR LIFE

If you step back and think about your life, you play many roles in it. At this juncture you are a graduate student, advisee, researcher, and perhaps a teacher in some capacity. Then there are many other nonacademic roles you may have, such as friend, daughter, son, mother, father, significant other (wife, husband, partner, girlfriend, boyfriend), volunteer, community member, or employee (many graduate students have full- or part-time jobs in addition to being graduate students and some even have faculty positions while they are completing their degrees). You may have other roles you consider important, such as cook, athlete, artist, board member, homeowner, aunt, uncle, grandchild, grandparent, or person of faith. I often ask my clients what roles they play in their life, and it is very interesting to hear their responses. They usually list some combination of the roles above with an emphasis on their roles and responsibilities in graduate school, as employees, and to their families. What is most striking is that not one client or student I have interviewed over the years has ever spoken of having a role as self-nurturer or self-caretaker. And many of these clients and students are in the fields of psychology and social work, where you might expect more self-awareness. Would you have listed a self-care role if I asked you what roles you play in your life?

When you stop and think about your life and the various roles you play, most of them are likely connected to meeting goals, academic performance, working toward your degree, taking care of others, and the general business of life. Those roles are certainly important and are central to your life. Accomplishing goals, contributing to others, and meeting your obligations can give you a sense of fulfillment, meaning, and even motivation to continue fulfilling your roles. But isn't there more to life? Being able to be your best in any of the roles you play in life requires that you attend to a role that is typically ignored: the role of self-nurturer or caretaker of the self (Ditzler, 1994). Taking great care of yourself lays the foundation for a balanced life in which your needs are met and you have the energy and motivation you need to be your best in your other important roles, such as being a graduate student.

It is important to consider whether you play the role of self-nurturer in your own life and whether you play it sufficiently. Are you meeting your own needs for rest, rejuvenation, and pleasure? I find that most graduate students have unknowingly put the role of self-nurturer on the back burner and have elevated the need to perform well and meet academic goals above other equally important personal needs. By thinking about the roles you play at this point, you can better consider whether you need to restore balance to your life and put the role of self-nurturer back on the front burner. I encourage you to consider what activities you would enjoy if self-nurturer was an important role in your life. What would you do more of? What would you start doing? What would you do less of? Attending to the role of self-nurturer and what you would specifically do to better fulfill that role can help you make self-care more of a life priority.

STRATEGY 2: CREATE YOUR OWN LIST OF SELF-CARE ACTIVITIES

If you are willing to adopt self-nurturer as one of your roles, the next step is to identify self-care activities that truly nurture and rejuvenate yourself. As you initially brainstorm your list, you may find it helpful to role-play someone who knows you well (e.g., a best friend, a spouse, a long-term dating partner, a close family member) and pretend that you are that person. Then, imagining that person's perspective on your life, list activities that he or she would know or sense would be really good for you. These would be activities that are relaxing, restorative, or fun.

Put down this book and try that exercise for at least 5 minutes. What did you come up with? List these activities in Step 1 of Exercise 8.1.

Some Surefire Activities to Get You Going

Let the time when you are in graduate school be a time to start tuning into your own needs instead of waiting until you earn your degree. In particular, I encourage you to consider the following activities as you develop your own list.

Physical Activity

First, I believe that some form of physical activity or exercise is important for graduate students. We all know that physical exercise is necessary for good health. It can also be an important antidote to stress (Byrne & Byrne, 1993). Research tells us that it is ideal to engage in cardiovascular and weight-bearing exercise on a regular basis (American College of Sports Medicine, 1998; Pate, 1995). If you can engage in both forms of exercise, you will likely benefit from each type of activity. What is more important, though, is that you exercise somehow in some way on a consistent basis. Whether you get out and walk, do exercise videos in your home, lift light dumbbells while you watch television, or ride your bicycle to campus, you are doing something positive for your health and well-being.

I know how challenging it can be to believe you have the time for exercise. When I am really working hard to meet a deadline, I take two or three 10-minute breaks in a day and run or walk briskly around the block or run up and down a flight of stairs in my home a few times. These short bursts of exercise are not sufficient for me in the long run, but I do get moving and obtain some stress relief. I encourage you to plan time for exercise in your action plan and look for opportunities in your day to move your body even for brief periods. Every bit of exercise makes a difference.

EXERCISE 8.1

Creating Your Own List of Self-Care Activities

Step 1. Imagine you are your best friend, spouse, long-term dating partner, or close family member and write down self-care activities this person would suggest for you at this point in your life.

_____   _____

_____   _____

_____   _____

_____   _____

_____   _____

_____   _____

Step 2. Now, be yourself again, and list some additional activities above.

If you are having difficulty identifying potential activities, you are not alone. By the time many of my clients have reached the dissertation phase of their academic career, they have forgotten what activities they enjoy. The act of brainstorming and writing your own list of self-care activities can be an important initial step to making these activities a priority (Domar & Dreher, 2000). What follows is a fairly sizeable list of possible self-care activities that I have cultivated from the lists made by my clients.

Examples of Self-Care Activities

Quick 5-minute meditation.
Practice deep breathing.
Do a few yoga postures.
Practice thinking positively.
Review rational coping statements.
Be compassionate.
Spend time with good friends.
Practice doing one thing at a time.
Read the newspaper.
Play air hockey or video games.
Watch my favorite TV show.
Eat mindfully.
Turn off my cell phone/e-mail.
Play guitar.
Lift weights.
Energize myself with fresh air.
Get a manicure or massage.
Go to the movies by myself
Take a nap.

Garden.
Take a hot bath.
Play basketball with friends.
Go to a museum.
Read spiritual books.
Read a novel (even just a chapter).
Go to the farmer's market.
Take a walk with no destination in mind.
Listen to great music.
Write in my journal.
Play with my cat or dog.
Brew great tea in a beautiful teapot.
Get a beer with friends.
Watch an old favorite movie.
See live music.
Work out at the gym.
Hire someone to clean my house.
Get takeout food after a tiring day.

Some of the self-care activities listed here take very little time, whereas some are more involved and require a bigger commitment of time, energy, and effort. Remember, self-care comes in all shapes and sizes.

Fuel Your Body in a Healthy Way

At the risk of sounding like your mother, it is important to eat healthy foods that make you feel good and to drink adequate amounts of water. I remember that my peers and I considered spaghetti sauce to be a vegetable and apple pie to be a fruit when we were in graduate school. We were not role models of good health. When you are a busy graduate student and short on time, getting to the grocery store and having time to plan and prepare healthy meals can be challenging. It is often easier to eat convenience foods that tend to be high in fat, sugar, and empty calories. When these kinds of food become predominant in your diet, you are likely to feel run down and to struggle to sustain the energy you to need to work effectively. If your diet is less than ideal, you do not need to fix it all at once. Start with small goals such as incorporating fresh fruit or vegetables into your diet once a day. Even an apple or a small salad each day can get you started on a path toward better eating. Dried fruit and nuts are highly portable and a great alternative to candy, chips, and other junk food when hunger strikes.

Another diet issue I have seen among many graduate students is drinking too much coffee or other caffeinated beverages. Our bodies need water to sustain alertness, so making sure you keep a bottle of fresh water around may help you avoid drinking excessive caffeine that can leave you dehydrated, unable to sleep, jittery, and anxious. Overall, I encourage you to focus on finding ways to gradually incorporate more healthy food and beverages in your diet. This approach is easier than aiming to drastically change your diet all at once. Tune in to how you feel as a result of what you eat and drink and allow that feeling to guide you to make better choices over time.

Spend Time With Friends and Family

Your friends and family can be a very important source of support and fun when you are in graduate school. It is all too easy to neglect these relationships when you are under pressure to perform academically. I encourage you to find ways to spend meaningful time with friends and family on a regular basis even if it just for an hour or two here and there. Time with friends and family can take your mind off your work and help you relax, laugh, and receive emotional support. It is okay to ask them for a break from the usual questions "How is your dissertation going?" and "Are you done yet?" Keep in mind that relationships with friends and family outside of the academic world can be an important way to help you keep things in perspective at a time when you life is so focused on academics. There is an important caveat to this suggestion. You may find that spending time with certain friends and family is more taxing than it is rewarding. So you may want to be cautious about who you spend time with and think about setting boundaries with people who drain you.

Ask for Help

A self-care strategy students tend to ignore is asking other people for help. You have a lot on your plate as a doctoral student, and it can be challenging to meet all of your obligations and fulfill all of your roles in life. Stop and examine your life and everything you are doing. Consider whether there is anyone you can ask for help. Can your significant other, a friend, or family member help you with meal preparation, childcare responsibilities, editing your work, or running a few errands for you during a crunch time? Is it worth spending a little extra money to hire some help? A few extra hours of babysitting for your children, hiring someone to clean your home or help with the laundry, or buying already prepared meals can be money well spent to help you have a little extra time and space to feel in control of your life. Remember, you are human and you have limits on how much you can realistically do. Asking for help so that you can reduce your responsibilities can be a great act of self-care.

Negative Activities That Masquerade as Self-Care

There is no right or wrong way to engage in self-care, with one exception. I caution you against engaging in activities that can be dangerous to you or someone else. For example, drinking alcohol is very dangerous if you drink excessively or drink and drive a vehicle. Consuming alcohol can also interfere with your ability to wake up and be productive the next day. Some graduate students use illicit drugs to relax and cope with stress. For obvious reasons, the use of illicit drugs is something I do not consider to be a good self-care activity. My intent is to encourage you to develop a responsible practice of self-care full of activities that you would find pleasurable, nurturing, relaxing, or restorative.

Continuing the Self-Care Brainstorm

Now that you have had the chance to read examples and consider some important areas of self-care, you can take some time to further brainstorm your own list of activities here in Exercise 8.2. Use your responses to Exercise 8.1 and the examples provided earlier to give you ideas. I encourage you to think about activities you can do when you do not have much time as well as when you have more time to invest in yourself.

EXERCISE 8.2

Continuing the Self-Care Brainstorm

Brainstorm your own list of self-care activities in the following categories: Activities that take (a) 15 minutes or less, (b) 1 hour or less, and (c) less than 1 day.

15 minutes or less

_____   _____

_____   _____

_____   _____

_____   _____

1 hour or less

_____   _____

_____   _____

_____   _____

_____   _____

1 day or less

_____   _____

_____   _____

_____   _____

_____   _____

Once you have completed your brainstorm of ideas, I encourage you to type your answers from Exercises 8.1 and 8.2 and make your own self-care list. Keep the list where you can refer to it frequently. In this way, you will be ready to make use of the next self-care strategy.

STRATEGY 3: PUT SELF-CARE IN YOUR ACTION PLAN

Each week when you create your action plan, consider when you will engage in academic endeavors and when you will engage in the self-care activities you identified in Exercises 8.1 and 8.2. As you create your plan, review your self-care list and purposively include time for those activities. In this way, your action plan can be a tool not only to help you make consistent progress on your dissertation but also to help you take better care of yourself. Planning ahead of time when you will work and when you will engage in self-care can increase the likelihood that you will make your needs a priority and enjoy the time you take off from your dissertation.

Some students express concern that if they start planning free time, there will be no spontaneity in their life. I agree that having spontaneous free time can be important, although I find that students who plan self-care activities are more likely to engage in these activities without guilt and that they do not miss spontaneity. Yet there is no rule that you must carefully plan all of your free time on your action plan. No one expects you to stick to your plan as if you are a robot with no needs or desires. If you spontaneously accept a dinner invitation, talk on the phone with a good friend for over an hour, or take an evening off, you can reexamine your action plan and adjust it accordingly. When you step fully into the role of project manager who takes responsibility for managing your energy and your dissertation, you can handle some spontaneous time off without it leading to days or weeks of procrastination.

STRATEGY 4: LOOK FOR SMALL OPPORTUNITIES TO ENGAGE IN SELF-CARE

One strategy to make self-care a more regular part of your life is to start taking advantage of small opportunities to relax and experience pleasure that you may be missing. I tell my clients to look for "cracks of time" in the day where they can wind down and experience pleasure. Self-care may be something as simple as taking a 10-minute break and getting outside for a short walk where you breathe in fresh air, are mindful of your surroundings, and remind yourself that there is life beyond your dissertation and earning a PhD. Perhaps the next time you eat a meal you could slow down and practice more fully tasting the food to help you be in the moment. A few minutes of deep breathing, a short call to a friend, a few yoga stretches in your living room, or listening to a favorite song can be simple ways for you to experience a little stress relief. Start looking for small opportunities to give yourself a break on a regular basis. Small acts of self-care can be a way to build up your entitlement to spending more time taking care of yourself in the future.

STRATEGY 5: ASK AND ANSWER KEY QUESTIONS RELATED TO SELF-CARE

Another way to help you develop a more regular practice of self-care is to ask and answer key questions related to making self-care a part of your life on a day-to-day basis. I often recommend that graduate students ask and answer the question, "What can I do today to experience joy and pleasure in my life?" I like this question because it focuses on what *you* can do (you are not relying on anyone other than yourself) to experience joy and pleasure. Also, asking and answering this question is about making self-care a priority today, no matter how busy you are, and developing a creative mind-set about how you can nurture yourself. The question above is focused on the here and now and is not about waiting until some perfect time in the future when you feel like engaging in self-care or when it seems like you will have the time. You can ask yourself this question in a variety of ways:

- Given everything I have to do today, how can I find a way to connect to life?
- Amidst all of this chaos, how can I use my creativity and intelligence to come up with some way to nurture myself and feel relaxed today?
- How can I find a way to be kind to myself today even though my thoughts tell me I don't have time to engage in self-care?
- What do I need today to help me feel more relaxed and at peace?
- How can I use my five senses to get present to life and be in the moment?

I encourage you to develop a habit of asking and answering some version of these questions to help you cultivate a rich, restorative, and meaningful self-care practice in your life now.

Too Much Self-Care?

A minority of graduate students feels they are too entitled to self-care. They tell me that they take too much time for pleasure, relaxation, and fun, and the absence of self-care time is not an issue for them. Their ability to make consistent progress suffers as a consequence of all this time they take for themselves. It is probably clear to you by now that I do not quarrel with a healthy sense of entitlement to fun and relaxation. At the same time, I recognize that finishing your dissertation needs to be a priority in your life if you want to earn a PhD. Certainly, you can decide to take your time and give yourself plenty of occasions for self-care while you are in graduate school. Yet it is important to have a balance between self-care and productive work time.

If you are someone who tends to take excessive amounts of time off and you want to finish your degree in the near future, you will need to shift the balance toward more time on your dissertation. Use your action plan as a way to plan meaningful time off from your dissertation to help you avoid feeling shortchanged on downtime. The knowledge that you have regular, planned time for yourself may help you focus and be more motivated when it comes time to actually work on your dissertation. View your action plan as a place to play around and determine the right balance of downtime and dissertation time for you given your coexisting need for self-care and productivity.

Sometimes the real reason a person takes too much time off from their dissertation is because they are avoiding the work they need to do.

Thus, they never say no to an invitation or opportunity for fun or relaxation. When faced with the challenge of working on their dissertation, nonacademic activities always seem more appealing. Who wouldn't rather go to a party, watch television, or spend time with a good friend than struggle reading dense literature, coding data, or interpreting research findings? If you tend to take too much time off, I strongly suggest you ask yourself the following three questions: Am I avoiding something? Is this activity another way to procrastinate? Do I realistically have the luxury of taking *more* time off at this point? If you answer "yes" to the first two questions and "no" to the third, then you will have to use self-discipline to forgo the immediate gratification of taking time off in favor of the longer term gratification of making progress and eventually finishing your dissertation. Do your best to be honest with yourself. Do you legitimately need some time for yourself, or are you using self-care activities to avoid doing work you find challenging, intimidating, or tedious? I trust that you instinctively know the difference.

Self-Care for Life

As you go forward, my hope is that you will make it a priority to consistently plan time to work on your dissertation each week and strive to stick to that schedule as best as you can. In concert with this effort, I hope you will deliberately plan time to take great care of yourself when you can relax, rejuvenate, and build your motivation to perform your best when you do engage in dissertation work. I encourage you to tune into yourself and recognize what is the optimum amount of self-care for you as you strive to successfully complete your dissertation. The efforts you make now will help set the stage for a postdoctoral life in which meeting your own needs and taking great care of yourself is a valued life priority.

A Final Word

I n many ways, the challenges you experience with your dissertation give you the opportunity to grow not only as an academic and professional but also as a human being. I believe that you as a graduate student have the power to take charge of your doctoral experience. No matter how you may have struggled academically, psychologically, and even physically up until the point you picked up this book, a new opportunity stands before you. Your graduate and dissertation experience can be a time when you deepen your relationship with your values and purpose in life. You can learn to become accepting of yourself and your experience of life; reconnect with your commitments to learn, achieve, and contribute; and boldly take action aligned with your most important goals and values. This is not necessarily an easy road you have chosen but it is a road well worth traveling. My hope is that you will take the tools and advice learned here to make it a more enjoyable and rewarding journey.

References

American College of Sports Medicine. (1998). The recommended quantity and quality of exercise for developing
and maintaining cardiorespiratory and muscular fitness,
and flexibility in healthy adults. *Medicine and Science in Sports
and Exercise, 30,* 975–991.

Antony, M. M., & Swinson, R. P. (1998). *When perfect isn't
good enough: Strategies for coping with perfectionism.* Oakland,
CA: New Harbinger.

Bair, C. R., & Haworth, J. G. (1999, November). *Doctoral student
attrition and persistence: A meta-synthesis of research.* Paper
presented at the Annual Meeting of the Association for the
Study of Higher Education, San Antonio, TX.

Beck, A. T. (1976). *Cognitive therapy and the emotional disorders.*
New York: Guilford Press.

Beck, J. (1995). *Cognitive therapy: Basics and beyond.* New York:
Guilford Press.

Bolker, J. (1998). *Writing your dissertation in fifteen minutes a
day.* New York: Henry Holt.

Bowen, W., & Rudenstine, N. (1992). *In pursuit of the Ph.D.*
Princeton, NJ: Princeton University Press.

Brach, T. (Author and Narrator). (2002). *Radical self-acceptance:
A Buddhist guide to freeing yourself from shame* (CD). Louisville,
CO: Sounds True.

Burns, D. D. (1980). *Feeling good: The new mood therapy.* New York: Avon Books.

Byrne A., & Byrne, D. G. (1993). The effect of exercise on depression, anxiety, and other mood states: A review. *Journal of Psychosomatic Research, 37,* 565–574.

Cone, J. D., & Foster, S. L. (2006). *Dissertations and theses from start to finish* (2nd ed.). Washington, DC: American Psychological Association.

Council of Graduate Schools. (2004). *Ph.D. completion and attrition: Policy, numbers, leadership, and next steps.* Washington, DC: Council of Graduate Schools.

Diffley, P. (2005, November). Selection and attrition. *Council of Graduate Schools Communicator, 38*(9). Retrieved from http://www.cgsnet.org/portals/0/pdf/Diffley%20Article.pdf

Ditzler, J. (1994). *Your best year yet.* New York: Warner Books.

Domar, A. D., & Dreher, H. (1996). *Healing mind, healthy woman.* New York: Dell.

Domar, A. D., & Dreher, H. (2000). *Self-nurture: Learning to care for yourself as effectively as you care for everyone else.* New York: Penguin Books.

Dweck, C. S. (1990). Motivation. In R. Glaser & A. Legold (Eds.), *Foundations for a cognitive psychology of education* (pp. 87–136). Hillsdale, NJ: Erlbaum.

Dweck, C. S. (2000). *Self-theories: Their role in motivation, personality, and development.* Philadelphia: Psychology Press.

Dweck, C. S. (2006). *Mindset: The new psychology of success.* New York: Random House.

Dweck, C. S., & Leggett, E. L. (1988). A social-cognitive approach to motivation and personality. *Psychological Review, 95,* 256–273.

Eifert, G. H., & Forsyth, J. P. (2005). *Acceptance and commitment therapy for anxiety disorders: A practitioner's guide to using mindfulness, acceptance, and values-based behavior change strategies.* Oakland, CA: New Harbinger.

Elliot, E. S., & Dweck, C. S. (1988). Goals: An approach to motivation and achievement. *Journal of Personality and Social Psychology, 54,* 5–12.

Ellis, A. (1994). *Reason and emotion in psychotherapy.* New York: Birch Lane Press.

Ellis, A. (2001). *Overcoming destructive beliefs, feelings, and behavior: New directions for rational emotive behavior therapy.* Amherst, NY: Prometheus Books.

Ellis, A., & Dryden, W. (1990). *The essential Albert Ellis.* New York: Springer Press.

Ellis, A., & MacLaren, C. (1998). *Rational emotive behavior therapy: A therapist's guide.* Atascadero, CA: Impact.

Hanh, T. N. (2003). *Creating true peace: Ending violence in yourself, your family, your community, and the world.* New York: Free Press.

Hayes, S. C. (2004). Acceptance and Commitment Therapy, relational frame theory, and the third wave of behavioral and cognitive therapies. *Behavior Therapy, 35,* 639–665.

Hayes, S. C., & Smith, S. (2005). *Get out of your mind and into your life: The new acceptance and commitment therapy.* Oakland, CA: New Harbinger.

Hayes, S. C., Strosahl, K. D., & Wilson, K. G. (1999). *Acceptance and commitment therapy: An experiential approach to behavior change.* New York: Guilford Press.

Hewitt, P. L., & Flett, G. L. (1991). Perfectionism in the self and social contexts: Conceptualization, assessment, and association with psychopathology. *Journal of Personality and Social Psychology, 60,* 456–470.

King, S. (2002). *On writing: A memoir of the craft.* New York: Pocket Books.

Knaus, W. (2002). *The procrastination workbook.* Oakland, CA: New Harbinger.

Lamott, A. (1994). *Bird by bird.* New York: Anchor Books.

Mullin R. E. (2000). *The new handbook of cognitive therapy techniques.* New York: Norton.

Pate, R. R. (1995). Physical activity and public health: A recommendation from the Centers for Disease Control and Prevention of the American College of Sports Medicine. *JAMA, 273,* 402–407.

Pion, G. M. (2001). *The early career progress of NRSA predoctoral trainees and fellows.* National Institute of Health Publications. No. 00-4900.

Rhodewalt, F. (1994). Conceptions of ability, achievement, goals, and individual differences in self-handicapping behavior: On the application of implicit theories. *Journal of Personality, 62,* 67–85.

Sapolsky, R. M. (1994). *Why zebras don't get ulcers: A guide to stress, stress-related diseases, and coping.* New York: W. H. Freeman.

Whitworth, L., Kimsey-House, K., Kimsey-House, H., & Sandahl, P. (2007). *Co-active coaching: New skills for coaching people towards success in work and life.* Mountain View, CA: Davies-Black.

Wright, J. (2006). *The soft addiction solution.* New York: Penguin Group.

Yale University. (1975). *Yale University Catalog.* New Haven, CT: Author.

Index

About the Author

Alison B. Miller, PhD, is the founder and owner of The Dissertation Coach, a business dedicated to helping graduate students earn doctoral and master's degrees. She has a PhD in clinical psychology from the University of Illinois at Chicago and a bachelor's degree in psychology from Cornell University. For her own dissertation study, she examined how the experience of homelessness influenced dignity and worth among homeless men and women living in shelters. She frequently leads dissertation workshops at universities around the United States. She is also the owner of Life Essentials, a company that offers life coaching and workshops. She lives in Chicago with her husband and two children. Alison can be contacted at http://www.thedissertationcoach.com.